PA
AU

"This book should be required in every high school civics class, book club, coffee shop, and bedside table—everywhere. It shows how close we in America are to the brink. Without raising his voice, Dr. Mack brings our peril straight home with authenticity, experience, and talented story-telling."

—Ellen Chaffee, PhD, University President Emerita

"This book should be required reading . . . especially for those of voting age. Ignore this book at your peril!"

—Margret Kramar, University of Kansas Faculty

"A concise and fact-driven survey of how dictatorships happen even in otherwise established countries, and why people have failed to stop it in time."

—Florence Brown, Magazine Editor (Ret.)

". . . an eclectic combination of memoir and political analysis. . . . astute and historically rigorous throughout. Mack couples his recollections with political commentary that assesses the terrible damage that autocracy does to civil society, and how an elected demagogue can nullify the very same democratic mechanism that ushered him into power . . . An often moving recollection of despotism and a lucid analysis of its genesis."

—Kirkus Reviews

PARALLELS
IN
AUTOCRACY

HOW
NATIONS
LOSE
THEIR
LIBERTY

WOLFGANG MACK, PhD

Parallels in Autocracy: How Nations Lose Their Liberty

For information about this title or to order other books and/or electronic media, contact the publisher:

WAMFAM Press
Mercer Island, WA 98040
wamfampress@gmail.com

ISBN-13: 978-0-578-63626-9
ISBN-10: 172-6344061

Library of Congress Control Number: 2018912909

Printed in the United States of America

Second Edition
All text © Wolfgang Mack 2018

Images by Wolfgang Mack or in the public domain
BISAC: Politics, Dictatorships, History

To our grandchildren, that they may not have to relive history because of their elders' complacency.

Also by this Author:

*Memories and Lessons of My Young Life
in Wartime Germany*

The Phases of Our Lives

In Search of a New Morality

ABOUT THIS BOOK

When our grandchildren were very young, they would ask typical children's questions, like "Opa, what was it like growing up in Germany, in the war, when people were so bad to each other?" And when I tried to explain these complicated things to the children they asked one question over and over—"WHY? Why did all this happen?" Their persistent "WHY?" made me think deeply about the underlying causes of Nazi tyranny, about issues of right and wrong in the politics of nations, and of basic human morality. My attempts to find answers grew far beyond the simple recounting of the facts of the story.

Later, when my wife Francesca and I took our grandchildren to the areas in Germany where I grew up, my stories became a lot more real to them. It also didn't hurt my credibility that they heard pretty much the same stories from my old friends there and my relatives. That was when it occurred to me to organize my thoughts in a book, so that when they grew up the lessons to be learned from the disasters caused by unprincipled national leaders would not be forgotten. It also drove me to be as historically factual as I could, because no inconsistency ever escapes a child's hypervigilant "fact checking."

Given this particular objective, it should not be surprising that I write about autocratic leadership—or, more specifically, about dictatorship—strictly from the perspective of my own personal experience. In other words, I want to convey to them what an "ordinary person" sees and feels when subjected to oppression and loss of personal freedom. I want to show them what living under a dictatorship does to people in their everyday lives, and how they have to learn to cope with daily threats to their personal liberty and the livelihood of their families.

I'd also like to state what my book is not meant to be. It is not an exhaustive study on the history of dictatorships—after all, I am not a political scientist, and I am not a historian. I do not try to grapple with the "big picture" of dictatorships—there are plenty of others who have done this exceedingly well. It is also not my intent to approach the subject of dictatorship in the light of our present party politics—I am not a politician. When I do make observations about our own country's present trends in national leadership I do not see them through the lens of parties or ideological groups—I see them as a matter of whether our elected representatives are doing their jobs properly, according to their oath of office which obliges them ". . . *to support and defend the Constitution . . . bearing true faith to it . . .*" I believe that regardless of party affiliation, all Americans basically have the best interests of our country at heart. However, that belief should not ever prevent us from asking questions when we see things happen on our political scene that make us doubt our leaders' commitment to the solemn oath to serve the people, and not their own personal interests.

But there is, indeed, one political message in this book—it is to remind all of us that our liberty and our democratic way of governing ourselves must never be taken for granted. Too many nations have fallen into the trap of complacency even when they could have seen the tell-tale signs of overly-ambitious politicians leading them into the national disaster that follows a slide into dictatorship.

CONTENTS

PART THREE   99
Our United States of America—Are We Immune to Dictatorship?

PROLOGUE

"Power corrupts.
Absolute power corrupts absolutely."

– Lord Acton, British politician and historian

What makes a "good" national leader?

"Sire, you need a person of great integrity and vision
of the Nation's goals, who can choose his objectives well
and after hearing all sides, can carry his determinations
decisively into action by connecting the institutions
and operations of government within the rule of Law.
However, I do not believe, Sir, that I am that person."

This is what Lord Frederick North is reported having said when his king asked him to become his prime minister. It was a most difficult period for Britain, the time of the American colonists rising up against England and the king. Whatever history may say about North's actions (or nonactions) his explanation of what would makes a good leader is right on. Adding that he did not think of himself as fully qualified, in fact, tells us that his political ambitions were tempered by a deep sense of responsibility to his nation. Though highly principled and knowledgeable, he also humbly recognized his own limitations. His king saw that North clearly understood what it takes to be a national leader, and North's display of humility made his king even more convinced that North had these rarest of leadership qualification: an understanding of his own limitations. He made North his trusted minister, never to be let down by him. Would we not want exactly that type of person as a national leader?

Why is it, then, that national leaders and the system of government they impose on their people so often have very different characteristics? We have names for those leaders that put their desire to dominate above the interests of their people. We call them by different names but they only differ in the degree by which they usurp control over the lives of the people in their nations:

Autocrat: One who has undisputed political influence or power and who believes that he can rule without the consent of others. *(Merriam Webster)*

Demagogue: A politician who exploits people's prejudices and fears to gain power with false claims and promises. *(New World Dictionary)*

Fascist: A follower of a political philosophy characterized by authoritarian views and a strong central government suppressing opposing opinions. *(Webster New Dictionary)*

Dictator: one ruling in absolute power and often in oppressive ways. *(Webster New Dictionary)*

Totalitarianism: A system of government where all institutions of political and civic life are made subject to the will of the dictator who alone decides on what is law and justice.

Leaders of nations have the chance to make history. Some do it well, many are just as well forgotten. Our history books give us a backward-looking consensus of how well leaders have done in the affairs of state, what they could have or should have done, and what missteps condemn them as failures.

But how well have they done for their citizens? Obviously, what national leaders do (or fail to do) will deeply affect the lives of their nation's ordinary people, especially when leaders use their power to force ideologies on their citizens, thus becoming what we refer to as dictators.

It is one thing to recount the "big picture" of what a dictatorship is all about and the disasters it always creates. But what about all the "ordinary people" who had to live through a dictatorship? How did they cope with oppression and persecution? How does an ordinary person deal with the dilemma when his own beliefs are different from the way he is now forced to live?

As a minimum, the result of dictatorship will be great spiritual and also physical discomfort for ordinary people, having to weigh over and over again the "pros and cons" of either resisting the dictator's demands or accepting them as inevitable. In an environment of personal freedom these decisions would be made based on a person's character. Under the threat of persecution, guidance by character will often have to be replaced by acquiescence, by a pragmatic weighing of personal benefits versus dire consequences.

Life under a dictatorship will deeply affect the very character of ordinary citizens. It can lead to permanent emotional and spiritual damage, or in the best case to a renewed hope for a better world. All this will come to fore once the dictatorship has collapsed under the weight of gross mismanagement of its nation's affairs. Then, to get the nation back to "normalcy" there will have to follow a period of reconciliation, as painful as it will be, because without it, the wounds inflicted by dictatorships will continue to fester forever.

Personal accounts of what actual people experience living under a dictatorship can be very useful to convey the seriousness of letting politicians gain too much control over their nations.

There are three stories to be told here—one of a boy growing up under a long-gone dictator who had not been stopped in time, then of several modern-day dictatorships in our Western World, and finally about the disquieting trends in our own country that are getting us further and further away from our ideals of governing ourselves in the democratic ways that have served our nation so well for so many generations.

Remember: *Every Demagogue is a potential Dictator*

PART ONE

*Germany's Descent
into Dictatorship*

"This then is the curse of one foul deed,
that it will always have to be followed by new ones,
in a never-ending cycle of violence."

– From Friedrich Schiller's Epic *Wallenstein*

WHAT I SAW
AS A YOUNG BOY

Every morning my buddy Helmut would ring our door bell to pick me up for our ten minute walk to school. Still chewing on my slice of dark bread I shouldered my backpack, and off we went to our next stop to pick up our friend Gunter to join us.

As we were waiting for him to come down, a woman came out from his apartment building, whispered to us that "they were taken last night" and then hurried away. Helmut and I looked at each other, with disbelief, shock, fear written all over our faces. We knew what this meant—we had heard rumors often enough about people disappearing in the middle of the night, never to be seen again.

But now it had happened right here, to our best friend and his family. Helmut started to cry. Shaken we went on our way to school.

Without our friend Gunter.

The war was in its third year. Up to now we had seen little of it, except that food had become more scarce and more soldiers were dying. My two older brothers were still writing to us from the Russian front, giving us hope.

But now with the Allied's air raids the war had come to our town. My classmates and I were only thirteen but we already had to do wartime after-school chores—cleaning up the rubble after air raids, helping to put out fires or collecting metals for the war effort. We were kept very busy but I could not get Gunter out of my mind. Where was he? What was happening to him? And why?

At school, I had trouble keeping my attention on my work. I could not stop staring at Gunter's empty desk. My homeroom teacher saw this. She said something like "Our country may need their help elsewhere in winning the war. In any case, they will be well taken care of—stop thinking about it!"

I guess this is what she was expected to say, but I knew better. My parents had told me that Gunter's family had been taken away because someone had denounced his father for having said something bad about the Nazis and about the war. I understood—even we youngsters were told in our compulsory "information sessions" that denouncing other people, even our parents, was our patriotic duty. My parents, of course, had warned me many times not ever to tell anyone what we were talking about at home.

So people simply stopped talking to each other for fear of being accused of something they said. Anything, even the slightest slip of the tongue could lead to disaster. As if the horrors of the air raids, the hushed-up bad news from the front, so many soldiers losing their lives in faraway lands were not enough—now we could not even be at peace in our own homes, with our family and friends.

But somehow, life had to go on. Together with my friends I did what boys would do—playing "cops and robbers," playing pranks on our neighbors, playing soccer, and running races. There was even the Nazis' version of the Boy Scouts, officially not compulsory, but if you did not join, you could no longer count on admission to higher education. As the war was coming closer to us, our "patriotic" indoctrination was becoming more and more intense. The ever-present fear of getting into trouble for not doing enough kept hanging over us like a dark cloud.

I now began to understand what my parents had been telling me all along about the Nazis leading our country into ruin. But it took a few more years of growing up for me to ask myself the much bigger question: how was it possible that my country would go down the path to dictatorship into ruthless oppression, to crass brutality, recklessly starting a war that would end in total chaos for so much of the world? How did this happen, of all places, here in Germany, a country once renowned for its great achievements in science, in culture, with its much envied institutions of higher learning?

Our beloved Germany had slid into a dictatorship, ruled unforgivingly by a band of nationalistic zealots, hell-bent on

7

imposing their contorted world view on our country, on the world. Law abiding as they were, many Germans submitted to their harsh rule especially after it had been given a semblance of legality.

How could this have happened in Germany, and why? It would take five years of the inferno of a world war and untold suffering for millions of innocent people for an answer to these haunting questions.

GERMANY'S ROAD TO
DICTATORSHIP

Two decades earlier the First World War finally had ended, not because one side was clearly the victor but because each warring country was exhausted—too many killed senselessly, too much wealth destroyed, too many going hungry, too many nations bankrupted. And then, far from trying to heal, the Versailles peace treaty opened new wounds, with Germany to carry the brunt.

After the war had ended, it would take Germany over ten years to find a new balance in its economic and political life. Finally, for the first time in its history Germany had become a democracy formally adopted in a constitutional convention held in the town of Weimar. But right from the start, its "Weimar Republic" was under attack from the extreme Left and Right, no party strong enough to garner a clear majority. In response to this reality the Weimar constitution provided that the party obtaining the most votes would be entitled to form the government. This meant that coalitions with other parties were always necessary, leading to the need to compromise, which in itself is not a bad thing.

In spite of their WWI postwar troubles, most Germans were gradually getting comfortable with their new democratic government. They began to look beyond the trauma of a lost war. The economy was beginning to recover, the devastating hyperinflation had wound down, people began to find jobs again. Things were looking up for them.

Until a wave of nationalism made Hitler their new leader.

Initially, Adolf Hitler's attempt to insert himself into the German political scene met mostly with disdain and contempt. After all, he was a total outsider, an Austrian and thus not even a German, with only rudimentary education, and certainly not a part of the ruling class. He had laid out his ideas in his book *Mein Kampf* to establish an authoritarian regime, to prepare Germany for war again, and declaring the Jews to be at the root of all problems. All this seemed so preposterous that most Germans were ready to dismiss him as a silly rabble-rouser. They came to regret it.

It would take Hitler twelve years of hateful oratory, an unending series of riotous rallies, and vicious street fighting by his private army to finally garner enough votes to make his party Germany's largest—but even after all this extreme campaigning no more than just 30 percent voting for him in Germany's last free election. However, under the Weimar constitution, this entitled him to form a new government which he did on January 30, 1933.

Much later, after all the damage had been done, many Germans asked themselves: How was it possible that a rogue like Hitler could wind up to be their leader, in a nation so steeped in tradition and valuing education and ethics as much as it did?

It turned out that Hitler succeeded precisely because he was not "one of theirs." Instead, he cunningly branded himself as the champion of all those who had been left behind in the German postwar recovery—the middle class that had lost its economic status, the workers who had been carrying the brunt of unemployment for too long, and, last but not least, the generals whose jobs had become obsolete after Germany's humiliating defeat.

On his march to become Germany's dictator Hitler used the same approach that had helped several other of his contemporary dictators. He was an eager student of how others had been able to elevate themselves into a position of absolute power. He saw that all of them had used similar programs—using demagoguery to create rabid followings of the dispossessed who would spread fear in the streets, intimidate judges, take control of the media, and then blame everything on some hapless minorities. Once in power they would generously hand out jobs to their followers to reward them with the possessions of those who had been eliminated for having opposed them. Hitler had seen how this basic program had been successfully used by every one of his contemporary dictators and he would use it too. Here is how he implemented it:

▸ Hitler was the consummate demagogue, a con artist and a compulsive liar, but his crude oratory and his outlandish promises appealed to the undereducated and the dispossessed. He was very, very good at it.

▸ With his mottos: "We will make Germany great again" and "Germany above All!" he also seduced many unsuspecting Germans into becoming his followers, blind to the deceit behind these slogans.

▸ Ignoring the legal process, Hitler immediately started to rule by executive orders, reducing Germany's legislative institutions to rubber-stamping his edicts. Government officials who dared criticize him were fired, and if they persisted, locked up.

▸ In rapid sequence he dismantled Germany's judicial system, dismissed dissenting judges, eliminated freedom of the press, outlawed all opposing organizations and labeled them "the enemy of the people."

▸ In a show of strength he proceeded to tear up international agreements that he found onerous. It endangered the country's security but made him popular with many Germans who felt their country had been unjustly humiliated.

▸ Next, he blamed minorities, foremost the Jews, for all the nation's problems, and ruthlessly persecuted them.

▶ When many Germans started to object to his trampling on all they held as their moral values he would tell them: "Look, I told you all along that I would do all this. I even wrote it in my book for all to read. You elected me anyway, so now stop complaining or else..!"

▶ When this was not enough to fend off his critics he did what dictators like to do—he started a war which would divert attention away from his Nazi goons' outrageous behavior ending any remaining opposition, all in the name of patriotism.

To seize power was one thing, but how would Hitler manage to keep it? From the beginning of his presidency he and his cronies were very much aware that the great majority of Germans were still very skeptical about his agenda. Many Germans hated his band of thugs that he had organized to keep opposition under constant threat of violence. But the more Hitler tried to assert himself in his still tenuous position the more Germans were determined to end his reign of terror.

He was driven by his fear that the Germans would eventually see through his deceit and would get rid of him just as they had done before with some of their political leaders. After all, he was very much aware that less than one-third of all Germans had voted for him in their last free election. And he was also alarmed by the growing opposition from his inner circle, the very men and women who had helped him to become Germany's leader. He knew he had to do something dramatic to secure himself in his newly obtained position of power.

So, in a move reminiscent of Stalin's purges Hitler had the leaders of his inner opposition killed. It sent shock waves through Germany.

How was Hitler able to get away, literally, with murder? How would he get away with the many horrendous crimes that he and his henchmen would commit in the years to come? He could do it because he had already "stacked" the courts with judges from his own party who predictably did nothing to prosecute him. Also, the German press was already controlled by Hitler's newly created Ministry of Propaganda which was spinning this purge as "the ultimate sacrifice for the good of the nation." For those who were still voicing their objection, his network of concentration camps was ready. Just enough about the atrocities committed there was leaked out in carefully measured doses, meant to spread terrible fear among Germany's population.

Seeing how he had escaped prosecution from that first massive crime spree, Hitler was ready to continue on his path of committing one heinous crime after the other, each aimed a consolidating his power, but each leading him—and Germany—deeper and deeper into the abyss, with one foul deed making the next one inevitable, a never-ending cycle of violence. It would take five years of a disastrous world war to bring an end to his heinous regime.

Hitler, of course, was keenly aware that many Germans still were just waiting for an opportunity to take him down—just a few years into his reign he had narrowly escaped several attempts on his life. (At least one of them, the one on November 8, 1939, was most likely a staged affair. It was carefully orchestrated to have Hitler leave the scene a few minutes earlier than planned, under the pretext of "scheduling changes" and thus escaping the big explosion. He would use it as a welcome pretext to unleash yet another sweeping purge of his opponents. Faking assassination attempts is a favorite ploy among dictators.)

Hitler then became paranoid about his own safety and responded to each crisis with ever escalating repression and cruelties with new repression, new violence, new killings of real or imagined challengers.

All dictators eventually will fall into this cycle of violence.

Driven by his paranoia, he and his inner circle developed a "bunker mentality" closing themselves off, trying to shield themselves from their own people. However, in doing this they also removed themselves from the realities of the life of their nation, causing them to make one bad decision after another.

Whatever his means, Hitler eventually succeeded beyond his wildest dreams—he had made himself the uncontested master of Germany. At this pinnacle of his career as politician you might assume that he would now settle into a new phase where he would begin to enjoy his position as the leader of a great nation, reluctantly acknowledged by the world as a reality to be reckoned with. However, like all men of great power he now became totally consumed with doing even more to secure his newly achieved exalted status.

He demanded everyone to swear an oath of unconditional loyalty to him personally. Those who would hesitate to do so would be eliminated one way or the other, from just getting fired or somehow disappearing—"accidents happen." With many Germans' exaggerated belief in the sacredness of a personal oath this made it so much easier for him to rule the country, unchallenged from other views about what would be good for the country.

But as a result, Hitler wound up surrounded with "yes-men," unwilling to give him contrarian advice for fear of offending his fragile ego. There was no one left in his inner circle to prevent their inexperienced "Commander-in-Chief" from committing one military blunder after another.

Then Hitler embarked on an all-out program to brand himself as a leader unmatched in history, as standing above everything and everybody, and especially above the Law. The personality cult he created for himself as Germany's *Führer* was aimed at making him unassailable in the eyes of his people, which is exactly what a dictator needs as a shield against any possible future challenge to his authority. Every schoolroom, every home, every government office was to display a portrait of Hitler. He required everyone to wear the insignia of the infamous swastika, the Nazi symbol of Aryan superiority that the Nazis had borrowed from ancient Hindu religions.

Keenly aware of the power of symbolism, Hitler made the Nazi swastika icon appear everywhere. Displaying the newly created German swastika flag became obligatory. Not to display this flag out your window would mark you immediately as an opponent, often with dire consequences. It would also immediately give the Nazi goons your location, for them to knock on your door. . . .

Was Hitler sincere in his misguided belief that he was the "savior" of his country, or was he just the typical pandering politician? Did he really believe all this stuff about his great love for the German nation, and all the venom he was spouting at his adversaries? Or was he a total cynic, simply tuning out, or even enjoying the monstrous crimes committed in his name? We may never really know.

But one thing is sure—every single step that Hitler took to eventually get complete control over his nation could have shown the Germans early on where he was heading. He became their dictator not by one single dramatic move, but in relatively small increments, one fateful small step at a time. Early on, at each one of these steps the Germans could have stopped him.

But they didn't.

THE LURE OF THE "GOOD ECONOMY"

Politicians know they will not stay in office long if the economy is not good. Not even the most debased dictatorship can survive if fathers cannot provide for their families and mothers cannot feed their children.

In order to get elected every candidate will be harping on the promise of jobs and good pay. For normal politicians any promise made during the campaign can be blissfully ignored once in office. But not for the aspiring dictator—doing away with unemployment, making the economy bustling again is the key to maintain his position of power. Whatever it takes he absolutely must make sure that everyone will have a job, with the best ones naturally going to his followers.

Promising "full employment" was a fail-safe way for Hitler to gain approval even from those who originally had opposed him. Even Germany's Socialists, originally among Hitler's most outspoken opponents, came around to quietly supporting him when they saw that he, indeed, had done away with unemployment within just a few years after taking over. Never mind that his way to ensure full employment was hugely destructive for the economy in the long run because he financed it by reckless deficit spending.

Dictators, of course, do not do this full employment bid out of compassion for the poor. They know that anyone who has been saved from the hardship and the humiliation of long periods of joblessness will be forever a grateful follower. Few of them will ever raise the question about the methods used to create their jobs. And few of them will ever realize that they are now totally beholden to their dictator—the specter of ever losing his job again will make almost every person submit to the most debasing action—anything not to lose the job, knowing that if he does not play along, he may never get a job again.

Anyone who just got a good job after years of unemployment is quite willing to overlook injustice and violence done to someone else, especially when he is told that this "someone else" is one of those "leeches of society" who the dictator's propaganda had painted as responsible for past unemployments.

And, most likely, in his new good job he will not even want to know about the real reason the job came into being—by the massive build-up of the military and armament programs camouflaged as "public works." It succeeded for a while, making things look up a little for the "man in the street" who began to see it as the "Great Hitler Economy." Little did they realize that sooner or later they would have to pay for it with inflation and with ever higher taxes as the nation was drowning in debt.

In their frantic efforts to stay ahead of national bankruptcy Hitler and his cronies resorted to more and more desperate measures, and ultimately to the disaster of World War II.

The edifice that dictators build is based on deceit and recklessness. Sooner or later, they will leave their nation bankrupt and their people will have to pay for it.

LIFE UNDER
A DICTATORSHIP

"The best political weapon is the weapon of terror, and often the threat alone of personal terror is even more effective than actually committing the terror deeds in themselves."

– Heinrich Himmler, Chief of Hitler's infamous Gestapo

From the safety of distance, in time and space, it's not difficult to trace the ways by which a nation can slide into dictatorship. The "big picture" is easy to see, but how about all the ordinary citizens? How do they feel about what is happening to them, how do they look at their government from their own personal perspective?

Their lives must, somehow, go on, even though they are very much aware that they have lost much of their personal freedom, and that they no longer can count on the protection by a reliable system of justice. But for most of them, their basic priorities have not changed—to have a family, to provide for them, to come home to them after the end of the workday, and maybe to spend some time with their friends.

Except for those Germans who joined the dictator's camp, life under Hitler's dictatorship was grim. You had to make decisions almost daily about how to deal with coercion and with blatant injustices, and often with frightening shows of brutality. What are you going to do when confronted with these realities? Are you coming to the defense of someone being beaten up right in front of you? Or do you turn the other way to avoid getting involved? What will either decision mean for you? What do you do when someone you knew had just disappeared? If you pursued the matter, you may well end up "disappearing" too. How does it feel when you realize there is no place where you can go for justice? You knew that you could not trust anyone. Whether you fully understood or not, all these daily pressures would affect your character, *and eventually the character of the entire nation.*

Everything becomes a matter of survival ensured only by conforming to whatever instructions come your way. The most successful of those who survive unharmed are those who have made themselves look as if they had fully identified with the system but in reality still harbor strong reservations. Actually, they are the ones dictators fears most—it makes them suspicious of hidden thoughts. Even those who have learned to hide their own feelings will go from one scare to another about the specter of being "interrogated."

The final effect is the loss of understanding of what is true and what is not, which relationship is honest and which is false. Once this has become a collective loss, the dictator has won. From that point on, everything can happen, even the most outrageous travesties of justice and morality. And so it did happen, to me, and to millions of others.

What we experienced in Nazi Germany was an "all-time high" in terror and barbarity, and an "all-time low" in morality. None of this came to us at once, all of it was slow in coming, one act of violence and injustice at a time. Did we ever get numb to it?

But as always, even in the worst of times, people turned to humor for some comic relief. It was the desperate kind of humor, mostly in the form of biting sarcasm.

One commonly told joke of those times goes like this:

After Hitler had already achieved complete control over everything, he organized another one of his sham elections which he "won" by 98.7 percent. His infamous police chief Heinrich Himmler came to him to celebrate this victory, saying "Think of it, only 1.3 percent of your people voted against you. What else could you possibly want, Great Leader?" Hitler's glum answer: "I want their names."

But getting caught telling jokes about the regime would surely land you in prison, or worse—dictators do not have a sense of humor. They cannot stand being laughed at.

Like all dictators, the Nazis just about perfected the many ways to blunt any remaining resistance to their regime. The threat of being hauled in for "interrogation" was already bad. Everyone knew what that would mean. The fear of winding up in concentration camp was enough to break the will of the strongest. We Germans knew that the camps existed, and we knew that they were awful, but few knew the full extent of their horrors until after the war. Another effective way to beat people into submission was to simply threaten to withhold food-rationing cards. Without a ration card, it was obviously impossible to live.

Then the Nazis introduced the particularly odious practice of *"Sippenhaft,"* making your relatives legally responsible for your actions. What a frightening thought that your father or mother or brother or sister could be hauled away for your alleged misdeeds! It was deliberately designed by the Nazis to say to the Germans: "Don't even think about resisting us!"

In another devilish move the Nazis abused a provision in the German legal codes that offered citizens the right to seek police protection if they felt threatened by others. They turned this right around and made it a tool of oppression. To get rid of critics of the regime they would engineer bogus threats on their lives and then "invite" their victims to enter the German protective custody system—in many cases never to be seen again. Then they would pin the "disappearance" on those they had used for the bogus death threat and got rid of those people too.

How did the Nazis get away with it? Simply because they had replaced all the important judges and prosecutors with those of their own party.

Denouncing others for real or trumped-up critical remarks was encouraged and happened all the time, with often dire consequences. It was another effective method of controlling the populace. Children denounced parents, businessmen denounced competitors, employees denounced rivals—treachery was everywhere. It was easy; any little whisper was enough to get you hauled in for "interrogation," and even if you were set free, you could be branded as an "enemy of the Vaterland." (To get a feel for this mentality, watch *The Lives of Others*, a movie set in postwar Communist East Germany. It could just as well have shown our life under the Nazi terror.)

By the way, do you know how Germans would greet each other during the Nazi regime? If you guess the infamous *"Heil Hitler,"* you are only partly right. Before saying "hello," or engaging someone in a conversation, you would furtively look back over your shoulder to see whether anyone else was close enough to eavesdrop on your conversation. This habit became second nature to many, and earned it the sardonic moniker, *"der deutsche Gruss"* (the German greeting). No joke. You simply could not trust anyone, period. Children were encouraged to inform on their parents, friends were set upon friends. The effect was utterly demoralizing.

For the average German, it was getting very complicated. Should all Germans have revolted at enormous risk for their and their families' existence? Where were the institutions, the leaders, who would have guided the Germans in such an effort?

Easy to judge from the perspective of a free nation that had never experienced political terror of this magnitude. But ask yourself, even with our civic freedoms still intact in our country, what are we in effect able or willing to do when we see abuse of power and injustice in our public life?

WHERE DO YOU GO
FOR HELP?

F aced with the ever-increasing oppression by the Nazi regime, many Germans were looking for political and emotional help from the nation's institutions. The first to disappoint the Germans in this search was the judiciary—the judges had sold themselves to the Nazis, just to be sure that they would keep their jobs (and their lives.) Any judges who continued to resist were replaced by those beholden to their Leader. The same with the public prosecutors—those that had remained in their position did not dare to risk their careers by bucking the Nazis.

Then we were looking to our military, traditionally an apolitical force claiming for themselves the highest standards of patriotism and honor. The military was dominated by the sons of the German aristocracy, who in addition to their position of power also had a high degree of financial independence—most of them came from rich landowner families in the North and East of the country, thus having the luxury of an escape hatch in case they would lose their jobs. To our terrible disappointment and to their everlasting shame many of these men turned out to be the worst cowards when confronted with the bullying by Hitler and the other Nazi goons.

That left the religious institutions. With very few exceptions, they, too, failed their flock miserably. We had witnessed the Catholic Church's reprehensible complicity with the Nazis, when saving its own position became more important than protecting its faithful. After all, the Vatican had made an odious agreement with Hitler, the infamous Concordat, by which the Church consented to stay quiet in exchange for the "guaranty" of safety of its clergy and the Church's property. From that point on the Church limited itself to insisting on doctrine and dogma rather than speaking out against the actual evil in the real world around it. We, of course, believed there were much more pressing problems than useless doctrines, like why eating meat on Fridays would land us in hell (most of the time there was no meat to eat anyway.) It would cause many Germans (and other Europeans) to take a critical view of our religious organizations' priorities.

In the end, stripped of useless trappings and senseless dogma, our religious life became more deeply spiritual, looking to its uplifting basic teachings, and simply trying to live by the Golden Rule:

"Do unto others as you would have them do unto you."

Where can one turn for safety and consolation if not even to our religious institutions, when you can not even open up to your spiritual advisor whom you are supposed to trust? It leaves you with a devastating feeling of loneliness, of hopelessness.

The one place you could hope to find support was your immediate family. But the Nazis had succeeded in sowing mistrust even there with their constant reminder that what was discussed within the family was not safe from scrutiny either.

Yet there were enduring friendships. Our neighbor around the corner was the principal of the elementary school, a burly man who was all authority, at least in our eyes. He was a highly decorated veteran of the first world war, in which he had lost his right arm. Their two daughters were in school with my sister and me, but a bit older. Our parents knew each other also from church, and they gradually developed enough confidence in each other to talk about all kind of matters that usually are only covered among the closest of friends. Our "victory garden" backed up to theirs, and occasionally we would go together to the countryside foraging for some extra food. But most of the time, we cautiously kept apart, like everyone else, not willing to risk a breach of trust.

But once we were invited into their home for a birthday party! At that time, being invited into someone else's home was something very rare, indeed.

There would be a party! A break from the dreary everyday fight for food, the never-ending air raid drills, the Nazi information meetings. Even writing about this seemingly little event some seventy-five years later, I get emotional about how much such a small social gathering had meant to us. How can anyone possibly understand who has not lived through periods like these?

For us at that time, it was a wondrous break in our dark war days. We were happy with any little thing that would bring us a light moment. Perhaps there would even be a small cake, a little juice, and for our parents perhaps a cup of "Ersatz" coffee. We knew not to expect much more. We, like they, had little to spare, but it didn't matter. My sister and I excitedly rehearsed the little poem we wanted to recite as our birthday present.

I still remember how they had decorated their home. Flowers everywhere, the table set with their fine china, an embroidered tablecloth and matching napkins—the *'gemüetlich'* German middle-class setting just as it should be. We sang, we recited poems, we drank, and we ate the delicious cake. Her father broke out the brandy he had saved for this occasion. Warmth and happiness all around.

Then the birthday girl stood up. Glowing with pride, she announced to her parents that she had signed up to join the *Lebensborn* to have a baby for her führer and the Vaterland.

For a moment there was stunned silence. It was as though we were frozen in our chairs. Her father glared at her trying to understand. "What did you say?" was all he could get out. Again: "What did you say?"

Not quite so sure of herself anymore, she said "Well, now that I am eighteen, I am able to do my duty to my country."

Her father and mother looked at each other in disbelief. Then all hell broke loose. Her mother cried hysterically, her father, red in the face, thundered "How could you do such a thing—are you out of your mind?"

He could not believe it. Here stood his daughter, in his eyes still his sweet little girl, in her youthful determination to do what her group leader had put into her head: You are to have a baby for your country from a true Aryan!

Her father would not have any of this. No way. "You go right now and tell your Leader that you are not going to do this, no way!"

Defiant, looking her father straight into the eye she yelled: "Nobody, not you, not anybody, will keep me from doing my duty! And I will tell my Leader what you said!"

At that, we all fell silent. Would she really denounce her parents? So many others had done this awful thing. Even my sister and I, then only thirteen and fourteen years old, knew what that meant—interrogations, stern warnings at best, and most likely a lot worse. Marked an *Enemy of the Vaterland* her father would be removed from his position, or worse, and then what?

The party was over. My father shook his friend's hand and looking into his eyes for a long moment, signaling his full support, as my mother gave her sobbing friend a warm embrace. There was nothing else we could do.

In their unfathomable immorality, the Nazis had created this Lebensborn in the middle of WWII in response to Germany's staggering human losses. It was an institution where soldiers meeting the Nazi criteria of the "Master Race" would be invited to impregnate young girls. Their babies would be given up to special orphanages to be raised to become good Nazis—and cannon fodder for future wars—a flagrant case of the State imposing its morbid concept of morality on brain-washed young people who simply no longer knew better.

Fortunately, what could have been an absolute horror ended well enough. She rescinded her decision to enter the Lebensborn, citing her commitment to nursing convalescent soldiers in the nearby military hospital. No doubt, her family's solid morality came through. Surely it also helped that she saw the same convictions in her neighbors. Contrary to what the rest of the world had thought at that time, not all Germans had lost their moral compass. Although the world found it hard to believe, many, many Germans held on their core beliefs in decency and personal honor, even in the face of the most ruthless oppression.

But it also shows again that dictators and their followers have this seemingly irresistible urge to interfere with the most personal of decisions people make about how to live their lives. They approach this complex field of personal choices with the zeal of an inquisitor, incensed by the idea that their citizens may have the audacity to make moral decisions on their own. Blinded by their righteousness the dictator and his followers will go to any extreme to interfere with even the most delicate personal preferences with unforgiving laws, followed by ruthless enforcement.

A leadership's irrational obsession with controlling the most private part of its people's lives is a clear sign of a dictatorship in the making.

THEN CAME THE WAR

"Of course, the people don't want war, neither in Russia nor in England nor in America, nor for that matter in Germany. That is understood. But the people can always be brought to do the bidding of their leaders. That is easy. All you have to do is tell them they are being attacked and denounce the pacifists for lack of patriotism, exposing the country to danger. It works the same in every country."

— Hermann Goering, Hitler's Field Marshal,
at the Nüernberg War Criminals Trials

On the First of September 1939, using as a pretext a faked border "incident," Germany invaded Poland, and thus started the inferno of the Second World War. In his campaign, and even in his manifesto *Mein Kampf* Hitler had said clearly that eventually he would take Poland's land by force.

Most historians of the Nazi regime are in agreement that the Nazis did not plunge themselves and the rest of the world into a devastating war just for the sake of making war—they did it under the pressures of dire economic necessities that they had created for themselves. After seven years of reckless government spending, Germany was nearly bankrupt. There was no money left to import much needed food from neighboring agricultural countries and, above all, no foreign exchange to import essential raw materials for Germany's weapons production. Also, there were more and more Germans grumbling about better working conditions, better pay and, above all, more affordable food. Taking Poland with its vast land resources, Hitler hoped, would solve Germany's food supply problem and silence for good what remained of the internal opposition.

Just to show how desperate Hitler was about the food supply crisis, imagine what it must have taken for him to make a nonaggression agreement with his great arch-enemy, Stalin's Soviet Union. All through his political career Hitler had derided Stalin and his "Bolshevik" regime as an abomination, as the ultimate threat to civilization, sparing no vile attack on Stalin and all Russians as "*Untermenschen*" (in the Nazi lexicon, the lowest of all human beings.) And to again show how desperate Hitler was, he even had to concede half of Poland to Russia as a price for their forbearance, who got all of that without even lifting a finger—some negotiating stance! Hitler then made his Minister of Propaganda, Joseph Goebbels, jump through hoops to justify this about-face to an increasingly confused German population that so far only had seen food scarcity and never-ending demands for more sacrifices for the sake of future glories.

But even after having paid handsomely for Stalin's complicity, Hitler's invasion of Poland was based on a huge miscalculation. He had assumed that the Allies would not come to Poland's aid as they actually were obligated under their mutual defense treaty. Why this risky assumption? Because Hitler had seen that in every one of his previous aggressions the Allies had not done anything to stop him when they could have done so quite easily. Here is what led Hitler to make his mistake that would change his and the Germans' lives forever:

Already two years into his reign many Germans had gotten impatient with Hitler. In spite of all the high-flying promises, life under his regime was not getting much better for them. Rearmament absorbed just about all of Germany's resources, pretty much depleting foreign currencies for imports making food scarce and expensive. There was a constant call for more and more "voluntary" services which left little time for family and friends. Hitler realized he had to do something to get his people to rally behind him again.

But there was also a pressing issue about where to get the raw materials for his huge rearmament program. Germany's main coal and iron deposits were in the western part of the country, but much of this area was occupied by the French under the infamous WWI Versailles peace treaty.

So, in his desperation to gain access to these vital resources, in March of 1936 Hitler ordered his army to throw out the French from the formerly German provinces west of the Rhine river. Hitler actually was gambling his entire future on the assumption that the French would not fight for fear of starting another major war; even though the French could have easily repulsed the German army which at that time was still quite small and ill equipped. He was also gambling that the Allies, even though obligated to help France would much rather not do so, again for fear of precipitating another major war. But in his desperation to hold on to his newly acquired power, Hitler knew he had no choice knowing that only if he would succeed with his gamble the Germans would follow him enthusiastically. They would see it as a great patriotic victory.

As he had hoped, the French decided not to fight and against everyone's expectations, the rest of the Allies also did nothing.

Now Hitler had finally become popular with just about all Germans. He had shown that Germany, indeed, was getting the world's respect again. Nobody seemed to understand how close his aggression had actually gotten them into yet another European war.

But even with the newly gained access to critical raw materials, Germany's financial resources continued to hemorrhage under the growing demands of rearmament and the huge cost of infrastructure projects that were actually preparations for war. Desperately looking around for new financial sources Hitler's rabid Jew baiters hatched a sinister plan: they would stir up public anger at German's wealthy Jewry, instigating a nationwide pogrom, the infamous *Kristallnacht*, aimed to frighten the German Jews to give up their wealth in return for the "right" to emigrate into safe countries.

Even with this ill-gotten "shot in the arm" Germany's finances were still in tatters. So, in March 1938 Hitler annexed Austria, immediately plundering his native country's financial resources. This did make the Allies nervous, and in September of the same year they came to ask Hitler not to seek further expansion. He readily agreed, never intending, of course, to honor this agreement. Naively, the Allies believed that they had secured " . . . Peace in our Time." But just a few months later, Hitler ordered his army to march into Czechoslovakia. This time it was not so much to make his Germans proud again but to get to the Czech's large gold reserves and to their significant armament industries. But even now that Hitler had shown the world that he had no intentions to honor any agreement that was not serving his purposes the Allies did nothing to defend the Czechs. Now Hitler had achieved his dream of making Germany really great again—from now on, Germany was to be called "Grossdeutschland."

So, after all these failures by the Allies to fulfill their contractual obligations to help their friend nations, Hitler concluded when he would take Poland, the Allies would again do nothing. But this time they did. They declared war on Germany and thus the Second World War got on its way.

Hitler and his cabal were dumbfounded. True, conquering Poland had given them what they were after—immediate access to its ample supply of food and workers and its treasury. Having been taken by surprise, defeating the Polish army had been easy, but Germany at that time was still woefully unprepared for a war with the combined forces of France and England. So, for the next six months, nothing much warlike was happening, except for some faraway naval skirmishes.

This was the time when Germany—and the Allies—could have easily stopped the war from getting out of hand but Hitler, the dictator, could not think about anything but raw power. For him, as for every other self-possessed politician, ensuring survival was the overarching interest—the country and its citizens be damned.

Just like warmongers anywhere, they had sold their war to the Germans as a somehow noble cause forced upon them by evil neighbors.

Of course, Hitler and his Nazi leaders had not been the first to use war as a way to safeguard their position of power. Every dictator's ploy is always the same—when things get tough for them because opposition challenges their mismanagement of national affairs they invent reasons to go to war. Under the motto "Rally around the Flag" they will paint all remaining opposition as "unpatriotic."

Unfortunately, this macabre ploy is not confined to outright dictatorships. Even some of the most democratically governed nations have not been able to resist the temptation to somehow invent a reason to get into war—preferably a war far away, in exotic lands, to lend an aura of "otherness" about the hapless people thus afflicted. It has happened in the best of democracies, *even in our very own,* because there always are politicians whose longing for war glory are too big for their conscience.

"It works the same in every country."

THE WAR HAD ENDED—BUT NOT OUR TROUBLES

Four years later, after inflicting immense human suffering, the enemies that Germany had created against itself finally put an end to the Nazi reign of terror. No matter what was one's political beliefs, losing the war was a terrible blow to every German's mind; seeing Germany so utterly destroyed and disgraced for all the horrors that it had inflicted on so many. They had known all along that the day of reckoning would be coming and that Germany would have to pay a huge price.

When it was all over, where were all these Nazis that had told us Germans to be brave and to sacrifice ourselves for their version of the Vaterland? They all had somehow disappeared into the miserable masses who were fleeing from the disaster that they had created. They were finally unmasked as what they really were—the most detestable hypocrites and cowards, ever, melting down to nothing the moment their Leader they had so adored had abandoned them—and their country. That much for the dictator's henchmen—when the chips are down, they are nowhere to be found.

It came as no surprise that Germany's former victim nations would extract more than their "pound of flesh" from Germany and the German people. Yes, the Allied victors had come to Europe as liberators, but that would not apply to Germany—they made it plenty clear that they were here to rule what was left of Germany by harsh martial law. To many Germans it seemed that not much had changed for them. It appeared to them as if they had just replaced one dictatorship for another one, albeit without the terror and the wholesale killings.

Against this background, was it so surprising that many Germans were doubtful about their victors' sincerity in reintroducing democracy to them?

It was left to those Germans who were the real patriots to deal with the mess the Nazis had left them. It was an almost impossible task under the harsh military occupation. These patriotic Germans tried very hard to get the best possible deals for their people by defusing some of the most onerous demands by the occupation forces.

And they were the ones who, against all the odds, eventually succeeded in getting their country back into the community of nations—but only after many years of herculean efforts to overcome the hatred and prejudices of Germany's former enemies. But they also had to face the bitter division between the Germans themselves, between those who would not let loose of their old Nazi dreams and those who were determined to find a new future for their nation.

This is when true patriotism is needed.

PART TWO

*How Do Nations Slide
into Dictatorships?*

"The greatest evil in this world is not just perpetrated by immoral leaders alone. The really dangerous ones are their followers who are told by their leaders that they are always right when they are doing their bidding. Those people know no mercy."

- Juli Zeh, German Humanist and Historian

HOW DO POLITICIANS MANAGE TO BECOME DICTATORS?

For sixteen of my growing-up years I had lived under the Hitler dictatorship, five of these years during the horrors of the Second World War, and then another three years under the harsh military rule of the Allied occupation forces.

With my first-hand experience of the disastrous outcome of Germany's dictatorship it is not surprising that I would watch with keen interest what happened during my lifetime in other countries that had also succumbed to dictatorships. Of course, at that time, (mid-1950s and 1960s) the threat of communist Russia under Stalin's ruthless rule was hanging over the world like a dark cloud and influenced just about every aspect of national life everywhere. In the two decades after the war, Russia established Soviet-style dictatorships in a number of countries. But there were also dictatorships not sponsored by Russia popping up during these cold war years in many smaller countries.

How do such dictatorships happen? Most of us think of a sudden military-style coup, with some rebellious generals plotting behind the gates of their military barracks to take over by sheer force of arms, sending their soldiers to storm government buildings, with guns ablaze. This is how dictatorships happen in unstable societies, in failed nations, typically in response to long periods of predatory governments. This was the setting of the 1917 Russian revolution, and Mao Zedong's "March on Beijing" and, on smaller scale, what Stroessner did in Paraguay, Pinochet in Chile, and Castro in Cuba. They all took advantage of some prolonged crises that had made their country fall into disarray, entering the political scene of their countries violently and with a lot of bloodshed.

But in countries with basically well-established civic and political institutions dictatorships do not happen that way. There, dictatorships come about in increments, in small steps which at the time they happen are often not even given much attention by the people, until one day they wake up and find that they had lost their freedoms, their protection under the Law, and if they chose to resist, even their lives. All this can happen at the hands of legitimately chosen national leaders who somehow evolve into dictators. What are the methods by which they succeed in overcoming the legal and political obstacles designed to prevent such power takeovers? Why do they inevitably wind up to become vicious oppressors of their people? And how do the people in such countries deal with having to live under a dictator's oppression and how do they eventually acquiesce?

How Do Politicians Manage to Become Dictators?

The example of Hitler shows how he had skillfully maneuvered around the restrictions put in his way by the German political and legal system of his days. Were his methods unique, or did aspiring dictators in other countries use more or less the same script? What are a country's conditions that make it ripe for dictatorship? Is every country different or can we see a pattern, some common threads, some kind of formula that politicians can use to get a country under their personal control?

I chose to take a closer look at four of the twentieth-century dictatorships to illustrate these similarities because I had first-hand experience with them—with Portugal's Salazar, Spain's Franco, Argentina's Peron, and Italy's Mussolini. I lived and worked in Portugal and in Spain and I did business in Argentina during their years of dictatorship. Then I worked in Italy a few years after the war when the Italians were still trying to pick up after the mess that Mussolini had made of their country.

I became especially familiar with the conditions that people in Portugal and in Spain had to deal with in their everyday lives under their dictatorships. As a young engineer I was delegated to guide Portuguese and Spanish government-sponsored programs to replace the old, uneconomical, single-use, wooden shipping crates with reusable plastic ones for their most important exports—fresh fruit and vegetables. In the 1960s these export products were the life blood of their struggling economies. (In their agricultural areas there was no adequate supply of suitable wood for the ever-increasing demand for shipping crates, and too much of the fruits and vegetables shipped in wooden crates would spoil on the way to their North European markets.)

Obviously, this assignment put me right into the middle of the delicate relationships between private organizations and their all-powerful government agencies. It showed me how difficult (and how dangerous) it was for the people I worked with to cope with all the uncertainties under their country's dictatorship.

Finding out more about the historic, big-picture aspects of these dictatorships is one thing. But I was most interested in hearing directly from the people I worked with. I wanted to know how it affected their personal lives, and how each one of them had to find a way to survive while trying to maintain their personal integrity when every little slip-up, every wrong word could land them in terrible troubles. Talking to me, a foreigner who they thought they could trust, they felt safe to open up. How could I ever forget how anxious they were to share their plight, but also how frightened they were that somehow it could get them in trouble. Needless to say, they had to be careful in all these conversations: "Big Brother is watching you!"

One morning the young engineer assigned to help me deal with the local growers' cooperative didn't show up for work. After the third day I asked about him but I met with only silence. None of his colleagues dared to start a search for him for fear that it could get them into trouble with the police and the local party thugs. Suddenly all the talk about the oppression they were suffering became a stark reality.

The man finally showed up again, unharmed. He had not been detained at all, just decided to take a few days off to visit some relatives in another town. The interesting lesson about this particular event was that you just kept quiet—a clear indication that the state's terror already had reached such a high level of intimidation—exactly as intended.

I remember very well what my Portuguese and my Spanish business associates thought about their national leaders. Each one of their dictators had started out quite normally as a part of his country's established political system. None of their dictators originally were rabble-rousers, each of them was well-educated and to varying degrees actually enjoyed a privileged upbringing. None of them set out in life planning to become a dictator, but all of them had at least one thing in common—an outsized ego.

In every case, what triggered their ascent into dictatorship was some kind of political or economic crisis, even a relatively minor one, to which they would respond with a messianic belief, a deep-seated conviction, *that they alone knew what was ailing their nation, and that they alone knew how to fix it.* It was this type of epiphany that would turn each one of them from an ordinary politician into an aspiring dictator. It is this messianic belief that is at the root of all the pains that a dictator is able to inflict on his people. It is the basis upon which a prospective dictator will sweep aside any scruples, any respect for his nation's institutions, and even its laws.

Still, even this all-consuming messianic belief is not enough to launch a politician on his path to domination. He needs to develop a large enough group of followers to transfer his messianic belief to make them into fanatics who unquestionably accept him as their leader. The way to do this is through good old-fashioned demagoguery.

Of course, every country has its own unique set of circumstance, and each of their leaders brought his own particular characteristics into their lives. My own experiences with Germany's dictatorship, and having worked in these four other dictatorship countries gave me a good understanding what methods each one of these dictators used to achieve domination of his country and how people had succumbed to their dictators. Studying these examples may be useful when we are contemplating whether, and how, future dictatorships could happen to other countries—*including our own.*

ANTONIO SALAZAR—
PORTUGAL

Antonio Salazar is the least known of these dictators but perhaps the most insidious one. After a distinguished career as economist he was elected to Portugal's parliament and named prime minister in 1932. He would rule his country for thirty-six years with "iron fists in velvet gloves." At the time he became the head of government, Portugal was just getting out from under a severe economic depression, with rich landowners pitted against their impoverished  peasants, wealthy merchants against their servant class. Under the motto "only unity can save our country" Salazar cunningly extracted one concession after another from his legislature until he was de facto Portugal's sole ruler.

His slogans were very effective. Who could find fault with his call for "unity?" To appeal to those who were demanding meaningful reforms he found another slogan, "The New State."

But then a brutal civil war was raging in neighboring Spain. Instigated by the Soviets, Spanish agitators began to unsettle Portugal as well, inciting riots and street fights and seriously disrupting the otherwise orderly Portuguese political life. In its desperation to prevent the Spanish civil war spilling over into their country the Portuguese parliament imposed some "temporary" restrictions on offensive news coverage. All publications were required to get a government license which could be revoked at any time. It did, in fact, helped to avert the country to sink into a civil war. It was a well-intended and effective measure at the time but its later abuse by Salazar turned out to become a disaster for Portugal for decades to come.

Once given the legal opportunity to restrict free expression the temptation for Salazar to use the press for his own political aims was just too great. With the constant threat of potentially losing their publishing license hanging above their heads the press readily consented to Salazar's demand that only his own editorials would be printed, in effect making the press into his own personal propaganda machine—a very shrewd move, avoiding outright censorship. Salazar understood perfectly that it would give him all the powers he needed to control just about every aspect of public life.

With the power of one-sided press coverage, Salazar proceeded to get rid of his opposition, eliminated dissenting workers unions, dismissed independent-thinking judges and government officials. Whoever did not abide would be sent to prisons, often in Portugal's African colonies, simply to disappear there.

So, what have we seen here? Salazar used four time-honored methods to gain, and to keep, his dictatorial powers: First, he selected the groups of dispossessed from each sector of Portugal's society as his standard bearers, eventually becoming his private police to enforce his edicts. Then he made the judiciary compliant by stacking the courts with his supporters. When he made his goons beat and kill opposition leaders, no court would prosecute him. Then he cunningly used the constitution as a tool to make the press do his bidding by forcing them to regularly publish his own editorials. But in spite of all these shenanigans everything was failing around him. So, in true dictator fashion, he started his Angola colonial war, effectively putting an end to all remaining opposition and appealing to the masses with his fantasy of "making Portugal a world power again."

But why, when he had already achieved such control over his country, did he resort to cruelly punish anyone who dared to oppose his measures? It was precisely because he was so convinced of the righteousness of his beliefs that he simply no longer had any tolerance for dissent of any type. As he resorted to more and more violence to enforce his edicts he began to see more and more threats to himself and his family, real or imagined, and responded with even more oppression. This is the trap that eventually all dictators fall into, even if they have started out with the best of intentions.

Historians sometimes classify Salazar as a "benevolent dictator." There is no such thing. Ask his opponents who languished in his horrific Angola prisons, and ask the thousands of families whose fathers, sons, and daughters disappeared.

In the judgment of the Portuguese people, decades after his demise, Salazar is given credit for having modernized government, having kept his country out of WWII and having put its economy back on the road of recovery, slowly but steadily improving the material lives of its people. But the Portuguese also remember the price they had to pay. Today, they ask themselves—was it all worth the pain, the agony, of thirty-six years of oppression?

FRANCISCO FRANCO—
SPAIN

General Francisco Franco had led Spain's ultra-right ("Loyalist") party to victory in the Spanish civil war. He was adored by the Right for his successes as their general, and hated by the Left for the atrocities that he condoned in his ruthless military campaigns—but as a result, he was perhaps the best known man in his time in Spain.

Shortly after the war had ended the Spanish Senate appointed him Head of State, in the hope that with his prestige as an eminent military leader he could bring peace to the badly fragmented Spanish polit-

ical landscape. As it turned out, General Franco found it surprisingly easy to grow into his new role as politician, moving with great speed to take a number of sensible steps to consolidate the new government. From the outset, the Senate had given him some extraordinary powers meant to help him deal swiftly with the country's huge economic and social ills.

Soon the Senate came to regret its generosity. Franco found it difficult to shed a general's deeply ingrained habit of making unilateral decisions—soon he would take on much more authority for himself than the Senate had meant to give him. With a general's arrogance, he had only contempt for civilian ways to govern. When the Senate tried to reign him in, he took his case to the ultra-right militia, the "Falange" who under his orders took to the streets, beating up any opponents and intimidating the courts. The Senate relented.

This is when Franco started to believe that "destiny" was showing him the way to Spain's salvation, that only he understood what really ailed his country, and that only he would know how to fix it—the quintessential belief system of budding dictators. Coupled with his general's mentality he was ready to take over.

As ambitious as he was, he did not have the makeup of a demagogue. As an orator, he was average, his speeches uninspiring. He deftly turned this limitation into his advantage by appearing as the calm and collected person, dispassionately and unselfishly having only the interests of his country at heart. Also, he never let people forget that he was a devout church-goer. Behind this image, however, lurked a man without scruples, hard and cynical.

He knew very well that in order to get complete control and to keep on top, he had to create a devoted following that would be ready to support him, no matter what. He knew his Spaniards—he reminded them of their two-thousand-year history, that at one time Spain ruled much of the world, and that he would make them "proud again of their heritage and their country."

To keep the image of the glory of old Spain in front of people at all times he promoted the "Falange" emblem. It was derived from the medieval Spanish royal coat of arms featuring arrows as a sign of military power held together by a duel oxen's yoke symbolizing unity and purpose. Franco revived it as his not-so-subtle icon of forced unity. To show support for Franco's Spain everyone was expected

to wear some form of this Falange icon. He made his Falange militia wear a military-style cap complete with the tassel and the Falange insignia.

The simple act of not wearing it was seen as a sign of opposition—often with dire consequences. Having to wear the dictator's symbol all the time also resulted in a form of self-reinforcing publicity—an effective way to create a personality cult, the stuff that all dictators love.

Franco told his people over and over that Spain's salvation required unity, and he coined the phrase "Unitary National Identity" to justify his increasingly oppressive rule. Partly to ensure the continued backing of the ultra-right he proceeded with banning all labor unions, outlawing all political parties and the free press, and replacing judges who had demonstrated independence. Anyone opposing his decrees would wind up in prison, in concentration camps, or would simply disappear. For the next twenty-eight years he would rule Spain as its undisputed dictator.

But why, after having already achieved almost complete control over his nation, did he become such a cruel despot? In the end, and in spite of his outward show of a general's bravado, deep under, Franco was a very insecure person. Knowing that given an opportunity his many enemies would be ready to take him down he developed an intricate system of surveillance, making everyone spy on everyone else, extracting information on real or imagined plots against him with elaborate torture techniques, in the fine tradition of the Spanish Inquisition. A failed attempt on his life gave him a renewed excuse for purging his real or perceived enemies.

(Irony of history—this particular assassination attempt was performed by an airplane dropping a bomb on Franco, something like a revenge for his infamous bombing attack on the town of Guernica by Franco's forces a few years earlier.)

Nothing was too base for Franco to assure him that he would stay in power—and stay alive. He lived in constant fear that his enemies would deal him the same horrible end of his life as he had so often dealt them.

Small of stature and with unimpressive looks his ego drove him to start an almost pathological personality cult, forcing the schools to teach the children that he had been sent by "Divine Providence" to save Spain from political chaos and from the people's poverty. But all while proclaiming his devotion to the nation's welfare he would secretly amass a huge fortune for himself and his family—over half-a-billion dollars worth of real estate and art, mostly expropriated from those he had sent to prison and to death as "Enemies of the Nation."

The Spanish Civil War had cost the lives of three hundred thousand soldiers. In the years following the war more than two hundred thousand civilians were murdered by Franco's right-wing militia, victims of their dictator's frantic efforts to stay in power at all cost. They were buried in two thousand mass graves, now officially identified and carefully mapped by today's Spanish government.

Today's Spaniards prefer not talk about the Franco era. For those who still remember, it is too painful a subject. In their schools, children are taught that it was an era of much confusion, of Spaniards fighting Spaniards, of political disunity that needed to be ended. Could this have been achieved by means less divisive, less cruel? Was it really necessary to put the country through such agony for eight years of civil war and then thirty-six years of oppression by a cruel dictator?

However, in history things are never as clear-cut as we sometimes want. There is one huge decision that Franco had made that offers some degree of "redeeming grace" in his otherwise dismal record—he managed to keep Spain out of WWII. Was it that even Franco had some remorse for all the horrors he had bestowed on his country during its civil war? Was it the mounting pressures from his people not to get into yet another war? Or was it even not his decision to make after all—was it simply that Hitler wanted the entire Iberian peninsula "neutral" so that the Allies would not land there—Hitler knew that the Allies would respect any country's neutrality even though he, Hitler, had demonstrated that he did not.

The Spaniards and the Portuguese will probably never know whether they really can give credit to their dictators for saving them from the horrors of the WWII catastrophe.

JUAN PERON—
ARGENTINA

Leaving his military career for politics, Juan Peron became Minister of Labor and then was elected three times as Prime Minister during the Cold War era that had put his country in the middle of Latin America's struggle against communist domination. As Labor Minister, he had made a name for himself as a strong proponent of reforms aimed at improving dismal working conditions and inadequate pay, especially for the unskilled farm labor-ers. As the "common man's president" his motto was "make Argentinians proud again to live here."

This approach resonated well. The country was stumbling from one economic crisis to another, with the added uncertainties about the festering border disputes with its unstable neighbors, Brazil, Paraguay, Bolivia, and Chile.

But unlike Spain's Franco, Peron had to campaign the regular way for his presidency. In fact, he had to do it three times, for three separate periods as president, to die in office in 1974. He was already well-known as an effective (leftist) advocate for labor and thus commanded a built-in lead over his centrist opponents. Then it occurred to him that the usual centrist-based government would be bound to fail again because it would always be faced with the two-front battle of the Center against the Left as well as against the Right, which had led to paralysis several times before.

So he hit upon a brand new way of getting his country to move forward—create a government that would be based on a coalition of the Left with the Right. At first sight this seemed to be an impossible dream but with his superb negotiating skills Peron, indeed, got these two opposing camps to work together. It resulted in a coalition of the workers (the Descamisados, "shirtless") and the establishment Right, especially its military. It would become known widely as the "Peronist Solution" to be emulated by other Latin American countries, however, with mixed results. But it was a shrewd move—with the workers on his side, Peron was assured of their votes, and with the military, if necessary, the force of their arms.

But even more important, Peron had succeeded in transferring his messianic belief in the good future for Argentina to his followers in both of these camps. His followers now were the ones to make sure, by hook or crook, that the other Argentinian political groups would succumb to their will. Peron had succeeded to make himself unassailable.

In his efforts to bring the dispossessed back into the mainstream of national life he got immense help from his wife Evita, soon to become even more popular than her husband. Whether by design or by the sheer force of her radiant personality, a new type of personality cult emerged—that of a "Golden Couple," selflessly nurturing their country back into peace and prosperity. It worked well for Peron, but the truth was elsewhere—as it became clear much later, Peron was not above enriching himself shamelessly at the expense of his fellow Argentinians.

Anyway, soon Argentina was well on its way to become an orderly country again, recognized widely as the best of Latin America. And he had achieved this remarkable feat without using force, to this point.

So why then did Peron start to use strong-arm tactics when he had already achieved his main goal by entirely legal means? Again, the answer is to be found in the seductive nature of a messianic belief that eventually will make a leader simply unable to tolerate any form of dissent.

After his celebrated success to put the Argentina economy back on a sound footing he fell for the temptation to eliminate anyone who would stand in his way. He had already fired several judges who were not among his supporters, and when his private "security forces" had beaten the editor of an opposition newspaper to death somehow no court was willing to prosecute the murderers.

Soon after Peron had gotten away with eliminating one opponent without legal consequences, full-scale persecutions were on their way, with thousands incarcerated, tortured hideously, and often simply disappearing. The more of this he did, the more it became clear to him that unless he would continue to dominate by sheer force of terror, he would find the same painful end as he was inflicting on so many others. His first foul deed had started him on a path of ever-escalating violence.

After all his initial good work Peron had joined the infamous ranks of dictators—a deplorable ending of an otherwise admirable life of service to his country. In the end, his messianic belief of his own superiority would negate the best of his original intentions and mar his otherwise splendid record as a leader who more than most had understood the needs of his people.

With their period of dictatorship way in the past Argentinians now have mixed feelings about Peron. They prefer not to talk about Peron's crimes but that Argentina had emerged from its nightmare a better country, a better society. For many the basic question still is hanging over them whether it was worth the many years of harsh rule, of street violence, of thousands of people disappearing. Above all, has Argentina learned enough from its years of oppression to make sure that it will never have to succumb to dictatorship again?

Now, some forty-five years after Peron's demise, the Argentinians are again facing economic and societal problems similar to the ones that got Peron into power. Quite a few Argentinians are clamoring for a "Peronist solution" to cure their current woes, conveniently ignoring the horrors that might come back, also. Those, anywhere in the world, who are basing their hopes on reviving their "good old days" should be reminded of the ancient wisdom that *"you can never set your foot twice in the same river . . ."* because with time passing neither the river nor yourself will ever be the same again.

BENITO MUSSOLINI—
ITALY

Just like Germany's Hitler, Benito Mussolini had become the head of Italy's democratic government through entirely legitimate means, and, just like Hitler, he never got more than one-third of the popular vote. But this made his party the biggest and under Italy's constitution that gave him the right to form a government. He became Italy's Prime Minister in 1922. Soon he would rule his country as dictator.

But it was not that he was imitating Hitler—it was the other way around. Hitler became Germany's leader a full decade later, and it was actually Hitler who saw Mussolini as his mentor. In fact, they became close personal friends, "two peas in a pod."

Of all the European countries, how would Italy ever succumb to a dictator, a country where the idea of enjoyment of life is quintessential, and where individuality always trumps the very idea of following any government rules?

Actually, at the time Mussolini became Prime Minister, Italy was ripe for major changes. Although Italy had been fighting alongside the Allies in the First World War it had been treated badly when the time came to share in the spoils of their victory. Italy's self-esteem was at an all-time low, its government institutions in disarray, its economy in shambles, crushing poverty everywhere.

Also there was the problem of the huge divide between the industrialized north of the country and its backward southern provinces with deep-seated cultural and societal differences that had not been resolved in the (then relatively recent) unification of Italy. It led to seemingly never-ending squabbles in Italy's legislature, resulting in political paralysis.

So, Italy was fertile grounds for massive changes. Four years into his political agitation, Mussolini had the future dictator's epiphany—that only he understood what really was ailing his country, and only he would be able to remedy it. He was ready to take control of the country. But how to do this in a country where blindly following a leader was not considered a good idea at all?

Mussolini was uniquely positioned for this task. In his earlier career as newspaper editor he had learned how to phrase stories to make them easily understood by audiences with very different levels of education. In his years in Italy's legislature he became very much aware of the difficulties to get groups with diverse interests come to agreements on anything. Above everything else, however, he saw that Italians of all economic and social levels had lost faith in their own country. Beyond the rampant poverty many Italians were deeply ashamed of their country. Nothing seemed to work— one government after another failing in rapid sequence, infrastructure crumbling, trains almost never on schedule. The country was bankrupt. No wonder so many Italians felt deeply humiliated.

Mussolini knew exactly what to do to get his compatriots out of this state of despair—he dug deep into Italy's glorious past, showing his people how their Roman ancestors once dominated the known world, how they brought law and order to unruly barbarians. In this vein he resurrected the ancient Roman symbol of authority, the "Lictorian Ax" and made it the official insignia of his party. It was proudly called the "Fascia" from the latin for "bundle"  meaning "everything held together in one," evoking the idea of national unity—and a not-so-subtle reminder that "the ax may come down on you if you do not follow our lead."

This symbol actually gave his movement its name: "Fascist," and it became the visual emblem of the new Italy. Italians had to wear the icon of Fascism all the time, and they had to display the fascist flag at every occasion. Not to do so would identify them as the "Enemy of the Nation" with the usual dire consequences. Soon, Mussolini's portrait had to appear everywhere. His personality cult was well on its way.

Next, Mussolini targeted the poor, the dispossessed, and by a flagrant misuse of public money organized them into his private political crack troops, the infamous "Black Shirts." He made them wear a martial-looking hat featuring the Lictorian Ax emblem, soon to be adopted by just about every Italian organization—a masterstroke of publicity. At his direction they would roam the streets, beat opponents into submission, and break up opposition meetings.

He used his Black Shirts to organize rallies all over the country where he would whip the crowds into a frenzy with his fiery and often bombastic rhetoric, mocking opponents with biting sarcasm, accompanied by often comical theatrics. Like an entertainer, he was thriving on the adoration by the masses, but more important, he used his charisma to transfer his messianic belief in a "New Italy" to his followers who then were willing to carry out any of his increasingly oppressive edicts.

After that, Mussolini's transition from Prime Minister to Italy's dictator was easy and almost unavoidable. But many Italians started to become restless as poverty and food shortages persisted. To divert his people's attention from their deprivations he did the typical dictator stunt—he started a war with the African country of Ethiopia. It was an ideal target. It fulfilled all the requirements to get his people's attention, evoking Italy's ancient past as a world empire, a country sufficiently weak to getting him a hopefully easy victory, and a faraway place with an indigenous population of a type that insinuated ideas of what we now call "white supremacy." The fact that things went horribly wrong was successfully turned into "resounding victory" by Mussolini's well tuned propaganda machine. His friend Hitler took good note of Mussolini's tactics, finding encouragement there for his own plans of aggression into Germany's neighbors.

To Mussolini's credit some of his programs to make Italy into a modern country again were hugely successful. The country recovered economically with almost full employment, its infrastructure vastly improved, trains running on time again. On the surface, Italy had come back. But behind the facade of success, Italy was financially bankrupt. Getting the economy going and creating millions of jobs with government money had exhausted its treasury.

Above all, it had come at a huge cost to personal freedom. Everyone now depended on the State for a job, for personal security, for access to education. In a way, all this was totally the opposite of what Italians traditionally appreciated so much in their personal lives. How could the Mussolini dictatorship have survived against this background?

It survived for almost twenty years because of increasingly brutal suppression of any opposition. Quite early in his rule, there had been three attempts on his life which he conveniently used as justification for Stalin-like purges, with any legal recourse squelched by the judges beholden to him. Only the agonies of the Second World War would finally make the Italians put an end to their Mussolini disaster, dealing him the same horrible death that he and his henchmen had so often dealt to his growing numbers of enemies.

It would take decades of very slow recovery to overcome his legacies. The jury is still out whether in the end anything good came out of Italy's dictatorship era. But it shows that even in a country with such strong preferences for individual personal liberties, dictatorship can happen if a demagogue succeeds in infecting enough of its people with his messianic bug.

What do Italians now say about their time under Mussolini? For most, all the agony and suffering during his dictatorship seems too far in the past to matter to them very much.

But their recurring comment is that if it could happen in a country as individualist as theirs, it could happen anywhere.

HOW DID ALL
THESE DICTATORS GET
THEIR START?

How can an overly ambitious politician even get started in taking the time-honored steps to make himself so powerful? Are there not some forms of "checks and balances" in every modern nation's constitution? Generally, yes, but all too often even in otherwise orderly countries there are always some weaknesses in their government set-up that a ruthless politician can exploit. No matter how thoughtfully a country's constitution is written, there are bound to be some clauses that politicians can use to amass more power that we want them to have. And unfortunately no matter how well structured a country's government set-up there are always some hidden flaws, some particular rules that can be abused.

In Hitler's Germany that weakness was that its constitution made it possible for Hitler to bypass the legislature in cases of "national emergency." By simply declaring a national emergency he could legally rule the country by "executive orders." In the case of Portugal, its constitution required newspapers to obtain a license. Under the threat of pulling their license Salazar could force the newspapers to publish only his own editorials. In Argentina it was Peron's ability as "Commander-in-Chief" to use the country's military to suppress his opposition, purposely provoking one case of violence after another to justify the use of their arms. In the case of Spain, the Catholic church had been made the de-facto state religion which enabled Franco to use the power of its pulpit to enforce his edicts. In Italy it was Mussolini's shrewdly playing the extremely diverse interests of the country's industrialized North against the agricultural and notoriously backward South ("Divide and Conquer!")

It is true that each of these dictators saw opportunities in periods of great social unrest in response to hyperinflation and economic collapse. You might think that economic pressures would lead to leftist (or communist) regimes but, interestingly, every western dictatorship that emerged from these upheavals turned to the extreme right, fed by a new wave of nationalism. Sometimes it was the various Christian religions that tipped the balance—they were more afraid of the godless communists than of the specter of right-wing oppression.

Dictator will spend inordinate amounts of money on the military and private militia for the personal protection. Corruption will be a huge drain on the nation's treasury, and so will be the endless rallies, carefully staged and choreographed to excite and entertain the masses. In every case I have seen, the countries under dictatorship wind up bankrupt after decades of financial mismanagement camouflaged by unsustainable deficit spending. In the end, it is the "common man" who has to pay for the years of inept dictatorship, his savings and property to becoming lost in hyperinflation and unfair taxation—a very high price to pay for the few exhilarating rallies and arousing speeches.

But even the most egocentric dictator needs to have people with some level of competence around him to make the government work. Could you not assume that at least some of them would try to keep their dictator from making serious mistakes that in the end could damage the nation and his regime, and potentially even threaten their own survival? At least some of his advisors are patriots and would want their country to succeed and not go down in flames due to their dictator's erratic decision-making.

The trouble is, of course, that autocratic leaders don't like criticism of any kind and therefore tend to surround themselves with subservient people. Even when the members of his team are competent in their fields of expertise they generally will prefer not to speak up for fear of losing their "place in the sun" or even worse, their lives. This leads to a self-reinforcing paralysis in the workings of government because it becomes preferable even in the lower ranks not to offer advice that those in command will find painful to accept. The result is a downward spiral into inefficiency, corruption, and finally loss of overall confidence in the future of the country.

All dictators lead their countries into bankruptcy.

What could have been done to stop these countries' descent into dictatorships? Just about everyone I questioned on this matter said that they simply had not paid enough attention to the first tell-tale signs that could have told them early on where their leaders were heading. In this sense, they all felt somehow responsible for having let their country's politicians get too much power. Once they saw how much of their freedom had been lost, it was too late.

HOW CAN NATIONS OVERCOME DICTATORSHIPS?

Eventually, all dictatorships come to an end. Just as their original causes vary depending on each country's situations their end comes in many different ways. Sometimes, it is peoples' inherent desire for some level of personal freedom and safety that many eventually create enough pressures for change from below. More often, however, dictatorships end as a result of outside pressures, either in the form of cataclysmic events, like a lost war, or from gradual but significant changes in the political make-up of neighboring countries. Ironically it is often the very disasters created by dictators themselves that finally will topple them.

However, one thing is true in all cases—no dictator ever will give up his autocratic rule by his own volition. No one can end this nightmare through a gradual and well-planned process. In addition the pains that come with ending a dictatorship can feel worse than the dictatorship itself, with new forms of violence by mobs hell-bent on revenge. That, of course, will eventually simmer down, and in the end the citizenry will come out ahead, way ahead.

What finally ended the five dictatorships that I had to experience myself varied very much—Germany's and Italy's as result of their cataclysmic defeat in a war they had precipitated, Argentina's largely because of the overreach of its military junta, and Portugal's and Spain's because the political climate in the rest of Europe had changed very much. Accordingly, they differ very much in their road back to "normalcy" from years of disastrous political lives.

Equally important, a closer look can also show us what their citizens had to go through to overcome their own personal trauma from years of living in constant fear and oppression. The scars from years of oppression, injustice, and plain terror are deep. It takes more than just a new more sensible government. There will be the painful confrontation with their fellow citizens who were the perpetrators of crimes. And even though revenge will be rampant, eventually there will have to be some form of reconciliation, as bitter that may be, because no nation can move forward while unresolved tensions from the past are marring their political lives.

Each of "my" dictatorship countries had to find their own ways to restore the faith of its citizens in themselves and in their nation. These countries' recovery processes teach us valuable lessons. We Americans should be thankful that we never had to live through a dictatorship. However, even a period of bad government will damage our country's self-respect and our standing in the world. Then we, too, may have to go through a similar recovery process to regain our confidence in our government and in ourselves.

HOW DID THE GERMANS MANAGE TO GET OVER THEIR NAZI DICTATORSHIP?

The cataclysmic end of the war left Germany deeply divided, not only in terms of the four separate military occupation zones but also in terms of those who were ready to face up to their defeat and those who were not ready yet let loose of their old Nazi fantasies. At first, things looked pretty bad. Many Germans were losing hope that they would ever be able to get back together and constructively deal with their awful legacies.

For four years after the war's end there was no more German central government, only local governments on a municipal level, and these were under strict control by the military. Many Germans were chafing at being reduced to helplessness by the humiliating and often repressive occupation forces. Those Germans who had not lost their senses wanted very badly to bring to justice their former Nazi leaders for all the horrors that their misdeeds had inflicted on them and the world around them. They were also deeply troubled about what to do with the many thousands of low-level Nazi thugs who had willingly lent their hand in enforcing their leaders' edicts with unbelievable cruelty, hideous torture, and wanton killings. How to do this without perpetuating the hatred between their former masters and those who were the real patriots?

Help came to the Germans from a totally unexpected place. The Allied occupiers did not trust the Germans to mete out justice on their former leaders and oppressors. Instead, the Allies insisted that only they, not the Germans themselves, would have the moral right and the power to do this. Accordingly, the famous Nuremberg War Crimes Tribunal was convened by the Allies, afterward leading to all kinds of questions on its legitimacy: "The victors wrote their own laws and applied them retroactively." In addition, they established that "just following orders from above" would not excuse the lower ranks from their responsibilities to behave like decent human beings.

Right or wrong, the Allies were shouldering the task of bringing these perpetrators to justice. By taking these thorny issues out of the hands of the Germans, the Allies inadvertently did them a huge favor by avoiding yet another deep division among the beaten-down Germans. They could now blame their occupiers for some of the controversial judgments they had rendered, deflecting potential finger-pointing among Germans. Once all the criticisms about the Nuremberg trials began to simmer down it made it much more possible for the Germans to start their slow process of gradual reconciliation aimed to overcome, in time, their deep internal schisms.

The bottom line was that the Allies were in effect doing the "dirty work," inadvertently relieving the Germans from having to shoulder the potentially divisive task of doing all this punitive work by themselves. In this way, the Germans could take out their frustrations and anger at the military government instead of at each other. It also helped to make the Germans acutely aware that they were in all this together, and that only by working together as a unit would they be able to eventually be able to get concessions from the Allied occupiers to gradually rebuild their own government structures.

It had been a long and arduous journey for the Germans. Nevertheless, the often painful reconciliation efforts have generated enough of a moral force to prevent any form of relapse into the authoritarian ways of their past.

We hope.

THE DISTURBING CASE
OF ARGENTINA

When their dictator Peron died, the country had spiraled back into economic distress and political chaos. Originally a remarkable success, his Left-Right governing coalition was falling apart. In true Latin American tradition, the military stepped in and established a dictatorship of their own, a "Junta," a group of ambitious generals. For the next eight years, they ruled the country with unprecedented harshness that elevated Peron's repressions to new heights of cruelty. Thousands of Argentinians were jailed, tortured, and then disappeared, just for speaking up against the Junta's crimes, or even just because they would not enthusiastically support it.

Argentinians who could fled the country. Those who could not despaired that their country would ever again be a place where they could live in peace and without fear. But even with the Junta's ruthless suppression, there was growing resistance.

And then, all of a sudden, and quite unexpectedly things changed almost overnight. The Junta had decided to take Britain's Falkland Islands, just off Argentina's South Atlantic coast, hoping that such a show of force would finally silence all remaining opposition. Precipitating a war is what dictators like to do when they feel threatened by growing resistance. The Junta thought Britain would not do much about their aggression, but it was a gross miscalculation. Britain's armed forces easily chased the Argentinians off the islands.

The Junta would not recover from this blow. In the eyes of the Argentinians, the Junta lost the aura of being all-powerful. The generals who had used their power so ruthlessly now looked like fools, and when the Argentinians rose up en masse to end their Junta's reign of terror, they found to their amazement that the army's rank and file no longer took up arms against them.

Within a few weeks their Junta was gone and replaced by a civilian government. It was confronted with the formidable task of bringing the nation back from over thirty years of cruel oppression and lawlessness. The new government asked itself the questions that all nations must ask after emerging for the nightmare of dictatorships—what to do about the perpetrators of crimes, how to help the survivors and the nation overcome their trauma and to heal their deep wounds.

In a startling turning away from the precedent-setting conclusions of the Nuremberg Trials, the Argentinians decided to charge only the "higher-ups" with the crimes committed during their years of dictatorship, not the lower ranks who had done their dirty work, invoking that "they merely were following orders." Dubbed the "Law of Due Obedience" it, in effect, excused the lower ranks of the army and the dreaded secret police and focused on prosecuting those who had given orders. This was a radical departure from the Nuremberg principles, but for the Argentinians it was more important to establish a framework for reconciliation rather than perpetuating their nation's polarization which had lead to rampant revenge killings.

As painful as this may have been for the survivors of the Argentina's years of terror in their "dirty war" it helped the Argentinians greatly to gradually overcome their resentments. For the next ten years they made honest efforts to find a new national sense of unity, and by and large, they succeeded in overcoming much of Peron's awful legacy. Unfortunately, after that period of relative internal peace the Argentinians had to face again one economic crisis after another, with sad relapses into civic unrest, even street violence and unjust incarceration of whoever happened to be on the wrong side of power politics. Today, the Argentinians live with painful "ups and downs" in their national life but at least they are free from the nightmare of outright dictatorship.

World opinion is still divided on the wisdom of the far-reaching legal concept of "Due Obedience Laws." They set a dangerous precedent that might even put into question some of the decisions by the present International Tribunal of the Hague in its persecutions of crimes against humanity. Recognizing the danger of its "two edged sword," the Argentinians decided in 2003 to repeal parts of this law, but its effectiveness in encouraging reconciliation to remedy past crimes is still being hotly debated.

SPAIN AND PORTUGAL—
LESSONS IN RECONCILIATION

After thirty-four years of ruling Portugal as dictator Salazar resigned due to failing health. For the next six years his successors tried with increasingly harsh measures to continue Salazar's "New Order" program until, finally, the Portuguese had enough and rebelled. To their great relief they discovered that the military, previously the regime's main tool of oppression, did not come out to march against them. Instead they joyfully accepted flowers from the rebellious protesters and even let them plant them into the muzzles of their rifles—hence the "Carnation Revolution." It ended over forty years of ruthless dictatorship without widespread bloodshed.

It was a change in other countries in Europe that made such an unusually peaceful outcome possible and even inevitable. By the time of its "Carnation Revolution" in 1974 most western European countries prospered in their democracies. They had become Portugal's all-important trading partners, and more and more foreigners vacationed in Portugal's resort towns, with many of them investing in vacation homes there. Needless to say, all this required some level of law and order. It became obvious that shows of violence and obvious injustices would put Portugal's new-found opportunities into question.

Throughout history, the Portuguese knew how to navigate the international scene—otherwise it would not have survived as an independent country, surrounded for many centuries with often hostile nations. This was not lost on all those Portuguese whose livelihood was now so tightly interconnected with their democratic customers countries. It was their self-interest that gave them the courage to rise up and to confront their past oppressors.

When they did rise up and found that the military was not fighting them the Portuguese also were ready to shelve most of their resolve to punish the perpetrators for their crimes committed under Salazar's dictatorship by a new program of "forgive but not forget." It helped stabilize the country in the eyes of the outside world but many citizens who had lost friends and relatives were clamoring for punishment of the perpetuators of these crimes.

Unexpectedly, help came from neighboring Spain, historically not always Portugal's best friend.

In his waning years, Franco decided to make true his dream of restoring Spain's monarchy by installing Prince Juan Carlos, a descendent of the old Bourbon dynasty as Head of

State. Franco had carefully groomed the prince to perpetuate his style of autocratic rule but to his great disappointment the prince, once put in office, turned out to be much more interested in following other European countries' leads in becoming democratic than perpetuating the "old regime."

In this vein Prince Juan strongly supported the groundswell of the "Pact of Forgiveness" movements that sprung up after Franco's death all over Spain—and then spilling over into neighboring Portugal. Under the motto "Let's restore the dignity of our nation" he succeeded in pulling together Spain's left and the right for the first time in more than three decades. On the strength of this remarkable achievement he limited prosecutions to the most egregious criminal acts committed under Franco.

Not every one in Spain was happy but in the end the prince's balanced views prevailed, saving his country from descending into another civil war. Partly to appease those hell-bent on revenge he established a commission for systematic mapping the mass graves of the victims of Franco's atrocities and to declare them National Shrines. As superficial as it may sound, it went a long way to ease the survivors' pain and helped Spain to become a fully functional democracy in a slow but peaceful process.

Eventually all dictatorships will fall under their own weight of mismanagement and cruelties, but their awful legacies can have long and bitter afterlives. It is the citizens' strength of character and their will to persist that will make the difference between continued strife and internal peace. But no matter how thoughtfully planned and how humanely conducted, even the best reconciliation program will leave indelible scars on victims and perpetrators alike. It is the unavoidable legacy of dictatorships.

PART THREE

Our United States of America—Are We
Immune to Dictatorship?

THE FOUNDATIONS OF OUR DEMOCRACY

Our nation's style of democracy has been for a very long time admired as the world's best possible form of government. It is anchored in our constitution that is seen as a model by many other countries.

Most of us are comfortable in our belief that our constitution and its concept of "Checks and Balances"in our government set-up are sufficient guaranties that we will always be able to live in freedom and safety from injustice, and that we will never have to face any form of autocratic rule by overly ambitious politicians. Yet, we must understand that no matter how well constitutions are written they are bound to contain some weaknesses, if only in wording, and no matter how carefully a government is structured, somebody looking for a loophole is bound to find one.

Again, remember the prime examples how in some countries budding dictators got their start by successfully exploiting such weaknesses:

- ▶ Hitler's systematical use of his constitutional power to rule by emergency edicts,

- ▶ Salazar's shrewed undermining free speech by abusing the media licensing requirements,

- ▶ Peron's unlimited authority over the military, or Franco making Spain's state religion into his propaganda channel.

Most of us find it hard to imagine that any such aberrations could ever happen in our own country. But do we, perhaps, also have some weaknesses, some imperfections in our constitution or in our particular government set-up, that overly ambitious politicians could use to grab more power than we want them to have? Our Founding Fathers made every effort to make sure that we would not have to face such possibilities, but have all their carefully phrased provisions remained relevant, some 230 years later, under the conditions of our present days that are so much different from theirs? Indeed, some of our constitution's provisions can only be understood if we look at the circumstances that our Founding Fathers had to face in their time.

For openers, each of the thirteen former colonies had very divergent interests which made it necessary for our Founding Fathers to make some very uncomfortable compromises just to ensure that all of them would join the Union. Several Articles of our constitution that we now find bothersome had their origin in the framers having to overcome objections based on very specific interests of some of the colonies in those days.

For example, when it came to voting rights, the southern slave-holding colonies had a very small voting population (the whites) and thus they were concerned that they would not get enough representatives into the proposed congress to take care of their interests. In order to entice these colonies to join the union, they were given additional weight in the form of "three-fifths" of the number of their slaves. Needless to say, for us today, this was an awful abomination. It was not until after the "Emancipation" many years later that it was finally eliminated from our constitution.

Another example is the allotting of two senators per each state, regardless of size or population. It was put into our constitution solely to entice the smaller New England colonies to join the Union because they were afraid that their interests would not be duly protected. This particular provision survived to this date, leading to the absurd situation that now five states with together less than 1 percent of our nation's population have the same number of senators (10) as the five most populous ones with over 40 percent of the nation's population. That alone would not be so onerous by itself but it is giving some less than responsible Senate leaders the opportunity to easily block legitimate Senate bills to serve narrow partisan interests. We have seen this happen over and over again, with Senate leaders openly bragging about the disruptive tactics made possible by the lopsided allocation of Senate seats.

No way could the Founding Fathers have foreseen that their "two senators per state" compromise would one day lead to such an imbalance of voting power in our all-powerful Senate. This is a striking example where a huge change in our nation's population has created new circumstances that made the original constitutional intent obsolete, justifying changing that particular provision to reflect today's realities.

Yet another provision that badly needs revision is our "Electoral College" which does the actual (indirect) electing of our president, regardless of the outcome of the (direct) popular vote. Our Electoral College is the brainchild of our elitists Founding Fathers who had a deep mistrust of the "common man's" ability to make informed decisions in such weighty matters. They were not entirely wrong because in their days many of the colonists were still illiterate and thus unable to inform themselves of political issues via written words. But there was another more mundane reason—in their times, communications were very difficult. The mail could take weeks, and travel was at the speed of a horse, in the best case. It made something like the Electoral College a practical response to the realities of their times. But in our today's circumstances, the realities of those days no longer exist, and therefore there is no more reason to hang on to this outdated artificial construct.

We should not just shrug our shoulders and say that we should just live with all these semisacred relics of times long past. We need to get rid of them because they could endanger the very existence of our democracy. But have these anachronisms done actual harm so far?

Yes, they have, and not in a small way at all. Our Electoral College has put doubts into the legitimacy of our presidential elections as it has several times already overridden the result of the popular vote, violating the principle of "one person, one vote." It is even possible that a determined minority could manipulate it to put into our highest office someone who should have no legitimate claim at all.

Similarly, the lopsided Senate allotments have provided a platform for the Senate to force ideology-based nominations of federal judges and important administration appointments. It has done so frequently in the recent past, causing legislative paralysis and a hardening of the partisan divide which has already poisoned our citizens' political dialogue.

Fortunately our Founding Fathers had foreseen the need for constitutional changes when our nation's circumstances would change over time. In fact, they even gave clear instruction how to do it (Article V). And sure enough, only two years into its ratification, they saw a need to make several amendments to set down in detail the protection of private citizens when confronted with the power of their government (the Bill of Rights). Then, over the years, one by one, seventeen more amendments were made to bring the constitution's original provisions in line with changed social and political concepts, like, for example, the abolition of slavery and the introduction of universal voting rights.

Clearly, those of our constitution's provisions that were largely the product of the particular circumstances of some 230 years ago must be revised and put in line with today's realities. For quite some time now many Americans (probably the majority) have seen clearly that something needs to be done to remedy these shortcomings. So, why do we not see any meaningful action? It is because the only ones who could do something about it are the very ones who have benefited from these anachronisms. Examples:

▸ Those representatives in our Congress that owe their position of power to the unconscionable gerrymandering of voting districts will most likely not demand more just voting district borders.

▸ A president who had lost by popular vote but squeezed into the White House only because of the machinations of the Electoral College is not very likely to support any effort to do away this anachronistic relic.

▸ Those senators who owe their disproportionate powers derived from the two-senators-per-state rule can hardly be expected to ever vote in favor of abolishing this totally undemocratic constitutional provision.

Thus we find ourselves in a procedural trap where only those who benefit from them have the power to change them. We can only hope that eventually our elected representatives will begin to put the interests of their constituents and their country above their own selfish exploitation of the privileges granted them by their electorate.

In these difficult disputes about updating some constitutional provisions we ultimately have to go back to the Declaration of Independence where our Founding Fathers stated unmistakably that *"all Men are created equal, that they are endowed by their Creator with certain unalienable Rights, that among these are Life, Liberty, and the Pursuit of Happiness. . . ."* This single sentence still must serve as the basis for any decision we make on our Constitution and the rules for our government that we deducted from it. It's actually quite simple—a constitutional provision is good when it fulfills what this sentence says, and bad when it doesn't.

THE POWERS OF OUR PRESIDENCY

*"The supreme quality of Leadership is Integrity,
essential for building Trust, which is the basis
for all relationships."*

– Dwight D. Eisenhower

Our Founding Fathers' attempts to define the office of
the future president led to their most heated discussion. On the one hand, they were deadly afraid of a possible
resurgence of some kind of monarchy with its absolutist
tendencies. After all, they had just risked everything in
fighting to rid themselves of the oppression by the British
monarchy. On the other hand, they were facing the stark
necessities of the mundane problems of communication
and travel—in their times, the mail would take weeks, and
travel was at best by the speed of a horse. That meant that a
lot of latitude had to be given the president to take decisive
actions in urgent matters when consultations and getting

approvals by other government members were not possible in a timely manner.

These communication issues were real problems in their times and are the main reasons why they finally decided to grant an extraordinary range of powers to the office of presidency. As a result our president can take a number of unilateral actions, for example, rule by decree after declaring a "national emergency," make or break international agreements, deploy the military, and hiring and firing the heads of government agencies. No other modern democracies are giving anywhere near as much power to their leaders.

Of course, our Constitution tried to curb presidential powers by the obligation to seek Senate approval, even after unilateral actions. In theory this should work well, but does it in today's real world of politics? What is the senate going to do when the president's actions have already created a "fait accompli" on the ground, that is essentially irreversible? What is our Senate going to do when the president declares a national emergency over some issue, real or fabricated, and then uses this as his justification to rule the country by "executive orders?"

One can say that this particular set of rules works well because we want to believe that the presidency is always occupied by a person of honor, by a patriot who always puts the interests of the nation above party doctrine or personal ambition. But even with all these assumptions, even the best intentioned presidency, like all of us, is subject to all-too-human imperfections. How can we protect ourselves when it turns out that some of our optimistic assumptions about the inner qualities of the president are put into question?

Most modern democracies' constitutions provide an elegant solution of this conundrum by having not just one single person to head the government but two: A president as head of state, representing the country, and then a prime minister for running the government. In this way, the concept of "checks and balances" is actually carried right into the country's ultimate leadership. Also, in this configuration, the president is expected to remain above party lines, serving as a sort of father figure for the nation. Many of the excessive powers of our president might be mitigated if we also adopted this two-person constellation.

We are for the most part comforted by our belief that any responsible occupant of our highest office will be wielding the extraordinary presidential powers only to further the legitimate interest of our nation. But what would protect us from a less honorable leader abusing these enormous powers? Will our "checks and balances" always do it when our Congress is consumed by partisan in-fighting?

Of course, we can always fall back on our judicial system to intervene in case of presidential overreach, right? But will we always be able to count on the impartiality of our judges when they have been selected not just for their judicial capabilities but also for their adherence to partisan ideology and even for their professed loyalty to the person of president?

It is not just the raw power of the president's office but also its moral leadership, its integrity, and trustworthiness that shape us in our daily lives and determines our nation's place in the community of the other nations.

WHAT MAKES A GOOD
PRESIDENT?

In order to prevail in the long run raw power must always be accompanied by exercising it with integrity so as to instill trust. The way our president acts determines how other nations perceive us, and whether our friends and allies will continue trusting in our leadership of the free world. No amount of raw power will be effective in securing other nations' friendship if we can not also convincingly demonstrate to them that we can be trusted to be a fair and dependable friend. It takes a lot of time to build trust, but trust can be very quickly lost if we fail to behave responsibly by the standards of common morality.

How did our past presidents stack up against these expectations? The forty-four presidents before our present one were very different types of personalities, with very diverse social backgrounds and levels of education. As you would expect from such a broad sample of ambitious men, all came to office with varying degrees of honesty and integrity.

But whatever their unique dispositions, all of them were striving to lend some level of dignity to their high office. Certainly, every one of them would take liberties from time to time with the truth when they felt it would further their ambitions, but they were ashamed or at least uncomfortable when they were called out for their lies.

Each one of them had big egos and wanted to be treated with deference, but most of them would give credit to others when due. They might, at one time or another, have wanted to be liked by the public for their personal traits but none really did too much to create a "personality cult."

Every one of them had their flaws, some more than others. Some were not liked for what they did, some were liked for perhaps the wrong reasons. However, all of them commanded respect, not only from their own citizens, but also from other nations. By and large, as presidents of our country, they made us Americans proud.

For better or for worse, our Constitution as it stands now gives our president huge powers, unmatched by those given to any other head of government in a modern democracy. For example, in our government set-up the Department of Justice reports directly to the president. By and large, this has worked quite well because historically our presidents have respected the huge importance to keep it truly independent from the politics or ideologies of the day.

But what if a president does not have the same respect for justice and would use his power to influence its decisions, for example, to punish his opponents? There are so many subtle (or not so subtle) ways for the many arms of our justice system to make life difficult for targeted citizens, like getting the IRS to do "tax audits" or calling off investigation into voter suppression if instructed to do so by the president, directly or indirectly.

We assume, of course, that the person we elevated to our nation's highest office would never do this, but what if it turned out that a president would not have the strength of character to resist the temptation to abuse his powers? It is not that easy to rebuild trust when we let down our friends in need of support, when we unilaterally tear up treaties, or abandon suppressed minorities' struggles for human rights.

The elusive quality of Trust makes all the difference in true leadership.

HOW TO CHOOSE
A "GOOD" LEADER

No nation has ever found a foolproof way to select the perfect leader for the right time. With all the imperfections of our American way to select our president it has, over the long history of our republic, served us pretty well, mostly.

What are the basic criteria that we should apply when looking at presidential candidates.? How can we assess whether a candidate will come through once elected? Is there something in the candidates' prior backgrounds that would give us a sure indication of qualification for this highest office?

Our often arduous election process is designed to make our candidates compete with each other so we can form an impression of the kind of persons they are, what they say about their ideas, and whether any one of them might make a "good" president. Alas, there is no easy way to predict who would make a good president. To begin with, there is no such a thing as a "President's Diploma" to be obtained by any kind of study course—for better or worse, it remains to be an "on-the-job-type" training that will show whether the person we voted for, in fact, turns out to be the leader we wanted.

Voters will, of course, have their own agendas and expectations, but when we strip away party ideology and personal prejudices, there are essentially three basic elements that we are (or should be) looking for—the candidate's vision where he plans to take the nation, the ability to actually run the government in all its complexity, and then the most elusive one, the potential as statesman, in the end perhaps the most important criteria of all.

The vision part is the easiest one—this is the stuff of campaign speeches, where candidates do all their promise-making and where their oratory and debating skills will make the difference in swaying the voters.

But how can we weigh each candidate's ability to actually run a hugely complex government structure? In the way we want to be governed, things get done by consensus or by compromise within the structures given by our constitution. But there are also the "norms" of actual running our government. These norms have evolved over many generations and are essential for the efficient running of our complex modern government. Ignoring these norms at best leads to loss of efficiency and at the worst, confusion and rivalry between government agencies, with one playing the other for primacy. This is why our president needs basic administrative skills and a knowledge of the inner workings of our government. That part should be learned before becoming president.

Finally, but perhaps most important, how about expectation for "statesmanship?" In a crisis (and crises will always come, for sure) it is this difficult-to-define quality of statesmanship that will make the difference for our success as a nation and whether other nations will follow our lead.

How well does all this play out in the realities of our often raucous presidential campaigns? We have the benefit of being able to look back at the track records of forty-five of our presidents, all very well documented. Did they have any particular personal traits that might give indication of how each one of them would succeed, would fail, or be judged as unremarkable? Why can't we simply elect a candidate on the strength of achievements in prior careers?

Let's take a look at our past presidents' backgrounds to find out whether a particular prior professional experience might have made the difference.

Some of us may say that a high military position would be a good training ground, with its discipline and rigid adherence to rules. George Washington had set a very high bar what military experience can do for the country, but after him only three of our forty-five presidents had come up through our military. With their proverbial disdain for the world of politics two of them were mediocre at best. One of them, Andrew Jackson, carried the general's concept of unilateral decision-making to such an extreme that his contemporaries dubbed him "King Jackson." Eisenhower was the exception, earning top rating but his most important work in his stellar military career was in what one can call "strategic diplomacy" coordinating the WWII efforts of a multitude of mostly difficult-to-handle allies. Undoubtedly, it was that skill as a diplomat, more than his military career as such, which gave him an excellent preparation for his presidency.

But how about candidates who amassed big fortunes in business? One argument says that at least they would not be tempted by corruption. President Hoover was one example of them but as president he was an unmitigated disaster, precipitating the Great Depression by his asinine decrees based in his own words on "his superb skill as a businessman." Another example of a wealthy president is our current one and the jury is still out on his legacy. But then, several of our best presidents, Lincoln and Truman had been total failures in business and yet became great presidents. They, like Wilson, were actually very poor and with that they also defied the preconceived idea that being poor would make them more susceptible to bribery—no one could have accused any of them of corruption!

So, success or failure in business is not a reliable indicator. What is left? Looking at our "good" past presidents we can see that just about all our successful ones had previously served in other leading government positions, as governors, senators, or cabinet members. This is where they learned valuable lessons in the basics of running governments, the art of compromise, and just how to get things done.

However, when we judge the performance of our past presidents we must also accept that success or failure did not solely depend on their personal or professional qualities but also on factors outside their control, like wars or economic crises. This is where the elusive quality of statesmanship comes into play, and there is no way to predict whether any person has the potential of this rarest of qualities once in office.

Beyond all that, the holder of our highest office and as a leader of the free world our president must create an aura of trust. Trust, this all-important quality in governance cannot be bestowed—it has to be earned. Creating this trust will be based on the president's personal character, foremost integrity and truthfulness. Trust is quickly and often irreparably lost when a president does not live up to these expectations.

This is not just a nicety—when trust in our president's integrity and dependability is lost, what chances do we then have that our friends and allies will stay with us? If our president unilaterally and willfully tears up international treaties, without good cause abandoned friends and allies in their time of need, if he insults other leaders, here and abroad, sidles up to cruel dictators with shameless flattery, then we cannot be surprised that the rest of the world will doubt whether there is any truth in our claims that we are the nation they can rely on in case of need.

TRUTH OR CONSEQUENCES?

"The liberty of the press is, indeed, essential to the nature of a free state."

– William Blackstone, British jurist and statesman, 1765

Our American way of life is best explained by our deep conviction that our personal liberties are fundamental to our existence as a nation. Nothing will shake us more than any attempt to tamper with our liberties, our personal freedoms, especially our right of free expression.

Our freedom of expression is enshrined in our constitution's First Amendment. Its language is crystal clear and requires no special interpretation—and yet our leaders every so often like to ignore it whenever it suits their particular purposes. It has turned into a perpetual 'tug of war' between government which often prefers to push back on uncomfortable publicity, and on our sources of public information.

Previous presidents have also had their fights with the press but none of them went to the extremes of calling the media "the enemy of the people"—that is the language we hear elsewhere from outright dictators. Relentlessly labeling legitimate reporting as "fake news" has already undermined our people's trust in the media and put confusion in our minds of what is true and what is patently false, as evidenced by the president's followers' Orwellian assertion that ". . . *only we have the facts . . . because we get them from our leaders . . .*"

As this would not be dangerous enough for our cherished free speech rights, we now find that there are serious attacks on this fundamental element of our democracy from the outside in the form of programs to systematically spread misinformation, and especially by interfering with our free election system. They are aided hugely by ubiquitous electronic communication capabilities and by the "social networks" that can so easily be manipulated into channels of gross misinformation.

We also seem to be getting numb to the almost daily spectacle of private interest groups openly pressuring our government and our legislature to do their bidding. Even our highest courts are not above bending our sacred democratic principles when they rule in favor of powerful interest groups whose declared purpose is to influence our lawmaking process—how else can you explain the blatantly undemocratic "Citizens United" ruling?

How are we to defend ourselves against these insidious erosions of our democracy? Of course, we should not allow this deterioration of our democratic principles to go unchallenged. We can certainly ask our "social networks" to do more to curb systematic misinformation especially if it comes from abroad.

Beyond that, is the answer some form of information control, or censorship, or declaring some technology-based anonymous publications illegal? This is a very slippery slope. Even with the best of intentions every nation that has tried to go down that path always ended in disaster.

THE CASE FOR A TRULY INDEPENDENT JUDICIARY

A truly independent judiciary is the most important guarantee for our freedoms.

In all modern societies there are three opposing forces to be kept in balance—the natural human interest to maximize personal freedom, the need of society to safeguard its interests, and for government to assert its authority. The judiciary's function is to keep these opposing interests in an often delicate balance.

When the judiciary fails to be impartial, or is hindered in doing its job, society breaks down, with either anarchy leading to chaos, or dictatorship leading to oppression.

We all want an independent and impartial judiciary, but what are we actually doing to make sure that we, in fact, have one?

The first thing, of course, is to put good laws on the books, but these are only as good as the judges who interpret and then apply them. So, a good part of having an independent and impartial system of justice depends on how we select our judges.

Surely, we assume that all those who have the power to appoint our highest judges will be guided by our belief that our justice system must always be kept independent of politics and ideologies. That is of eminent importance for the rule of law that we expect and that our Constitution meant to enshrine.

Unfortunately, our realities are often quite different. In our system, federal judges and prosecutors are nominated by the president. Every president who is given an opportunity to fill court vacancies will try to place judges who most likely will side with him in his decision-making, thus trying to "stack" the courts in his favor. His nominees will then be vetted by Congress and are approved mostly along party lines. By definition, this means the process by which we appoint our federal judges is essentially a political one, not one limited to considerations of jurisprudence. The lopsided composition of our Senate has become the vehicle for many of our our federal judges being appointed not for their eminence as jurists but for their willingness to pledge loyalty to the president and his party ideology.

Is that a good thing, and is that what we, the citizens, really want? It is hard to imagine that this is what our Founding Fathers would have wanted. This flagrant violation of the concept of judicial impartiality extends also to every level of federal judges. For example, our current president has openly been bragging that he successfully placed over one hundred new federal judges that were chosen primarily based on their conforming to his ideologies. To top it all, he added that he deliberately chose unusually young candidates in order to make sure that his brand of "conservatism" will be guaranteed to prevail for many years after this administration.

In essence, by stacking courts with judges along the lines of ideology, the courts would be set not just to *interpret* the Law, which is what courts should do, but to, in fact, *legislate from the bench*. Thus, even our Supreme Court is set on a path to becoming just another political body meant to do the president's bidding.

In most modern democracies, in order to eliminate the undue influence of politics or ideology, the selection and placement of higher judges is done differently. Their judges are appointed by panels of fellow jurists strictly on grounds of their competence and reputation as jurists.

For example, in England, judges are selected by the "Judicial Appointment Commission" which is a nonpolitical body composed of jurists appointed in turn by England's equivalent of our American Bar Association. In France, high court judges are appointed by the President of the Republic on recommendations of the Higher Council of the Judiciary which is explicitly prohibiting any form of political or ideological influence.

And with their disastrous past history still haunting them, the Germans have gone to an extreme not to repeat the huge mistake that had enabled the Nazis to pervert their judiciary. Germany now has instituted a two-tier process selecting superior court judges by an independent panel of jurists overseen by the ministry of justice. These then have to pass muster by yet another committee formed partly by members of the German constitutional court and partly by the candidates' peers in the districts where they had been working before.

Selecting justices on the basis of their personal beliefs and ideologies is an insidious attack on the integrity of our judicial system. Should we not be concerned about how far we have already gone away from our reliance on the independence for judiciary? Should we not be alarmed that large parts of our public have shown a disturbing indifference to this huge departure from what our Founding Fathers fought so hard for?

Never in our country's long history have our highest courts been politicized to such a degree. As a result, how can we still hope for impartial justice? But most disturbing of all, where is the outrage among our citizens over these flagrant distortions of our justice system? Where is the outrage when the White House reaches into the workings of its Justice Department to squash legal proceedings that are not to its liking, or instructs it to reverse otherwise unchallenged convictions? Has our voting public already become so numb to this flagrant undermining of our judiciary's independence?

The outside world has for very long been looking at our American democratic ways as a prime example of good governance. It will take a huge effort by all of us Americans to stop the present slide into lawlessness and to reestablish our and the world's confidence in ourselves and our democratic institutions. As a first step, let us make sure that our judiciary will once again become a truly independent and unbiased institution. Without that, we will surely be heading further down the road to less and less liberty and into period of governance by leaders that no longer respect the supremacy of the law.

SAVING OUR DEMOCRACY

We Americans love our country, and because we do, we want to make sure that the principles that make our country great are protected.

We Americans believe in our country, and because we do, true patriots do not stand idly by when our freedoms are threatened.

We Americans respect our system of government, and because we do, we want to make sure that it will not be hijacked by militant ideologies.

We Americans take pride in our institutions, and because we do, we want to make sure that they will be always there to serve all of us—equally, and with justice for all.

The unfortunate reality is that there are disturbing signs that our great democracy is under active attack from many sides, both domestic and foreign.

Many of us are deeply concerned with the growing politicization of our judiciary, with the relentless attacks on the free exercise of the First Amendment. We see our legislative process stymied by extreme partisanship and the use of arcane procedural rules to push through unyielding ideological creeds. As citizens who love this great nation, we need to work together to counter these threats.

We should not shy away from amending those parts of our constitution that are so clearly outdated that they present a threat to the practice and health of our democracy. Also, there are numerous loopholes in our government structure that present dangerous openings for unscrupulous politicians to assume more power than we are ready to grant them. For the sake of the future of American democracy, we need to take action to correct these imperfections.

Most of us hesitate to suggest changes to our Constitution, even when some of its provisions no longer reflect the realities of modern times. But did our Founding Fathers think that the Constitution would be unalterable, to be taken verbatim, sacrosanct for all ages? Of course not. They understood perfectly well that as time would pass, and as their newly formed nation would evolve, there would be a continuing need to update the framework for the way we govern ourselves.

Accordingly, they provided the tools in the Constitution itself to do this. But, in their wisdom they also required "supermajorities" to ensure that changes would not be made casually, to accommodate every whim in the fickle winds of politics. Quite on purpose, they made sure that constitutional changes are hard to make.

This is a good thing, but should not be used by our politicians as an excuse to shirk their duty when outdated provisions threaten the very foundations of our democracy. Certainly, most of us want to see the Electoral College eliminated, making way for the sacred principle of "one person, one vote." No one really believes that the lop-sided senator allocations serve the country well. Few of us are comfortable with the growing threat to the independence of our judiciary, the one institution that, in the past we, the citizens, could rely on to protect us all equally. These are clear and present threats to the future of our democracy.

Constitutional amendments are hard to enact, but there are a number of problems that can be dealt with more readily. Congress has the power to stop—and reverse—the politicization of our judiciary, the pernicious voter suppression schemes practiced in many states, and laws like "Citizens United" that allow corporate money to control legislation. It is entirely within the rights of Congress to do away with arcane senate rules that are routinely exploited by irresponsible politicians to further their selfish aims.

Also, there is nothing in the constitution that tells us about how many Supreme Court Justices we have to have, and whether they have to serve for life. Same for senators and house representatives—setting term limitations is entirely within the capabilities of our Congress. Changes like these would go a long way to safeguard our democracy against entrenched interests of self-serving politicians.

Whoever will have the great honor and the huge responsibility of leading our country in the future will face the formidable task of bringing outdated provisions of our Constitution and undemocratic government rules into harmony with the demands of our times. Will our leadership have the courage and strength of conviction to tackle the pernicious obstacles that the entrenched special interests will put in their way?

Predictably, the attempts to make these hugely important changes will meet with resistance by those of our politicians who owe their positions of power to these untenable rules. But if they really love our country, if they really meant it when they swore their oath of office, then they must put patriotic duty above personal ambition. When we see them fail in these duties, they need to be voted out and replaced by candidates who are truly committed to the oath of office they take.

The outside world has long looked to our American democratic system as a prime example of good governance. It will take a huge effort by all of us Americans to stop the present trend in the direction of authoritarianism and to re-establish our (and the world's) confidence in ourselves and our democratic institutions. If we fail at this task, we are bound to lose what so many have fought for throughout our nation's history. The fear of this loss of liberty is precisely what drove our Founding Fathers to establish our constitutional framework of government. In the eternally famous words of Benjamin Franklin: *"we gave you a republic . . . if you can keep it!"*

EPILOGUE

The ancient Greeks invented democracy as a way to live in freedom, pushing back despotism that had been the accepted political structure for centuries. It lasted while they continued to fight for their liberty. They fell back into despotism when they had become complacent.

Ever since then people everywhere have been in a never-ending struggle trying to defend their natural longing to live in freedom against those who want to dominate them. In our own times, the parties in this perpetual fight are the modern democracies on one side and the dictatorships on the other, with all kinds of variations of autocracy in between.

Where in this spectrum of political systems are we? Are we heading into a direction of a better democracy, or are we heading in the other direction, into a more authoritarian one? What are the directions we see in our present leaders?

We Americans believe that we are secure in our democratic ways, in our freedoms. Most of us have faith in the decency of our compatriots and in the basic fairness of our political system, and these beliefs give us justification to hope that our country will not ever veer off into an authoritarian form of government.

This faith in the stability of our government concept, however, should not lead us into complacency. We need to be vigilant and act decisively at the first signs of our politicians grabbing more power than we are comfortable giving them. Have we already become accustomed to glaringly undemocratic ways as the "new normal" in our political discourse? Is there still time to stop this ominous trend or are we too far gone already to reset the course for our country back to a better democracy, and not further down the path to a more authoritarian one?

In the end, it falls on each of us, citizens of the best democracy the world has ever seen, to defend our liberties. Remember: Liberty is not free—it needs constant participation by all of us to keep it alive. The first defense, as in all democracies, is the ballot box. When we do not make full use of it, we are letting ourselves down and we are opening our nation for all kinds of attacks, from within and from the outside.

It's up to each one of us!

ABOUT THE AUTHOR

Growing up in Nazi Germany, Wolfgang Mack witnessed his country's slide into the nightmare of a dictatorship the likes of which the world had never seen. After barely surviving the war he studied engineering and economics in Germany and Austria, and under a postgraduate Fulbright scholarship in the US, settling eventually here with his young family.

He has managed industrial enterprises here, as well as in countries while they were still reeling under dictatorships. Working closely with their professionals under often trying circumstances gave him a good understanding what it means for ordinary people to live in an autocracy.

Later, representing industry associations in our halls of politicians and lawmakers he also gained insight in the ways interest groups influence public policy making. He has lectured on these subjects and served on several business and nonprofit boards.

He now lives in Seattle, Washington, married to his wife Francesca for more than fifty years, enjoying their four sons and their families, and above all their eleven grandchildren who give special meaning to their lives.